Geomancy

For Beginners

About Richard Webster

Author of over forty titles published with Llewellyn, Richard Webster is one of New Zealand's most prolific writers. His best-selling books include *Spirit Guides & Angel Guardians*, *Creative Visualization for Beginners*, *Soul Mates*, *Is Your Pet Psychic?*, *Practical Guide to Past-Life Memories*, *Astral Travel for Beginners*, *Miracles*, and the four-book series on archangels: *Michael*, *Gabriel*, *Raphael*, and *Uriel*.

A noted psychic, Richard is a member of the National Guild of Hypnotherapists (USA), the Association of Professional Hypnotherapists and Parapsychologists (UK), the International Registry of Professional Hypnotherapists (Canada), and the Psychotherapy and Hypnotherapy Institute of New Zealand. When not touring, he resides in New Zealand with his wife and family.

Geomancy

For Beginners

Simple Techniques for Earth Divination

RICHARD WEBSTER

Llewellyn Publications
Woodbury, Minnesota

First Edition
First Printing, 2011

Cover photograph © Lynne Menturweck
Cover design by Adrienne Zimiga

Llewellyn Publications is a registered trademark of Llewellyn Worldwide Ltd.

Library of Congress Cataloging-in-Publication Data
Webster, Richard, 1946–
  Geomancy for beginners : simple techniques for Earth divination /
Richard Webster.
      p.   cm.
  Includes bibliographical references and index.
  ISBN 978-0-7387-2316-7
  1. Geomancy. 2. Divination. I. Title. II. Title: Simple techniques
for Earth divination.
  BF1773.W43 2011
  133.3'33—dc22
                                    2010036627

Llewellyn Worldwide Ltd. does not participate in, endorse, or have any authority or responsibility concerning private business transactions between our authors and the public.
  All mail addressed to the author is forwarded, but the publisher cannot, unless specifically instructed by the author, give out an address or phone number.
  Any Internet references contained in this work are current at publication time, but the publisher cannot guarantee that a specific location will continue to be maintained. Please refer to the publisher's website for links to authors' websites and other sources.

Llewellyn Publications
A Division of Llewellyn Worldwide Ltd.
2143 Wooddale Drive
Woodbury, MN 55125-2989
www.llewellyn.com

Printed in the United States of America

Also by Richard Webster

contents

introduction

When I was twenty-one, the publishing company I worked for sent me to the English county of Cornwall as a sales representative. I was excited, as this gave me a territory of my own and a company car. My landlady was extremely interested in psychic matters, and introduced me to a wide range of people with similar interests. This was exciting for me, as up until then I'd had to keep my interest in the psychic world a secret.

Back in the 1960s it was almost a guilty secret to be interested in these subjects. I had been educated at a Christian school, and then worked for a company that published a large number of Christian books. I'd found myself in trouble at school because of my interests in palmistry and hypnosis. Consequently, I'd learned not to discuss anything to do with psychic matters outside of my immediate family.

Suddenly, thanks to my landlady, I met dozens of people with similar interests. One of the groups I joined studied different forms of divination using gemstones. I loved the look of the crystals and the beautiful displays they made. I also enjoyed making my own divination stones from stones I collected on a riverbank. Henry, one of the members, helped me make my first set of rune stones and taught me how to use them.

At one of the meetings, Henry mentioned rune sticks and the art of geomancy. This was the first time I heard the word *geomancy*. We all asked him to bring his rune sticks to the next meeting. I was slightly disappointed when he produced four sticks, each with one line on one side and two lines on the other. However, I was immediately captivated when he demonstrated them to us. I was amazed that such a simple process could produce such detailed and accurate readings. We all made sets of rune sticks and enjoyed working with them, using the method described in chapter 10 of this book, Arthurian divination.

I used my rune sticks regularly, and many of the clients who came to me for a palmistry reading received an Arthurian divination reading as well. About ten years after I first learned about geomancy, my sister gave me a copy of Stephen Skinner's *The Oracle of Geomancy* as a Christmas present, and I discovered there was much more to the subject than I had imagined. I have been involved with geomancy for more than forty years, and I am still learning.

The word *geomancy* comes from the Greek word *geomanteia*. *Geo* means "earth," and *manteia* (-mancy) relates to divination. Consequently, geomancy is the art of divination from the earth. Geomancy, in a variety of forms, is one of the oldest methods of divination, and its origins are lost to time.

Not surprisingly, a number of legends try to explain how and where geomancy originated. The Arabs say that Jibril (Archangel Gabriel) taught geomancy to their prophet Idris (Hermes Trismegistus) after he saw the angel drawing a geomantic figure in a dream. When Idris asked for enlightenment, Jibril taught him the basics of geomancy. Idris passed this information on to an Indian king called Tumtum al-Hindi, who later wrote a book on the subject. This book was kept secret for many generations until it came into the possession of Khalaf al-Barbari. When Khalaf was converted to Islam, the prophet Muhammad told him that earlier prophets knew all about geomancy, and if someone studied it diligently, he or she would "know all that the prophet knew."

Another legend about the origins of geomancy also involves Idris. Idris could not find any work, and prayed to God for a way to make a living. Shortly after this, Idris, still unemployed, was aimlessly drawing figures in the sand when a stranger asked him what he was doing. Idris replied that he was actually doing nothing, and was drawing the figures purely to amuse himself. The stranger laughed at this, and told Idris that he was doing something extremely important and useful. Idris doubted this, until the stranger explained the meanings of all the figures Idris had drawn. He asked Idris to draw another figure, which he also interpreted. This continued until Idris had drawn all sixteen of the geomantic figures. The stranger then taught him every detail and nuance of geomancy. Once he was certain that Idris knew everything there was to know about geomancy, the stranger told Idris that he was the angel Jibril, and then disappeared.

In his book *Summa Breviloquium*, Bartholomew of Parma (fl. late thirteenth century) wrote that geomancy had a divine origin. According to his book, God asked an angel to take on human form and teach the art of geomancy to the sons of Noah.

Historic records show that geomancy dates back at least three thousand years, as the ancient Chaldeans were known to use it.[1] As the original names of the sixteen figures used in geomancy were traditionally said in Arabic, it is possible geomancy began in Arabia. Geomancy is mentioned in a number of ancient Greek and Roman manuscripts, but unfortunately none of them include descriptions of the techniques they were using. One reference describes how Archimedes (c. 278–c. 212 BCE) made figures in the sand to determine the outcome of a battle during the siege of Syracuse. This was obviously geomancy, but unfortunately not enough detail exists to work out exactly what he was doing.

Geomancy, as we know it today, was refined by the Arabs in the eighth century, and was known as *Raml*, which comes from *'ilm al-raml*, "the science of sand." During the ninth and tenth centuries, Islam expanded into West Africa and introduced geomancy there. *Fa* and *Ifa* divination, which is what geomancy is called in Africa, is still a highly regarded and popular form of divination in that part of the world. Geomancy was also introduced to Madagascar in the ninth century, where it is known as *Sikidy*.

During the twelfth century, the Arabs introduced geomancy to Islamic Spain, and from there it quickly spread throughout Europe. This was helped by the publication of two books on the subject in Latin, *Ars Geomantiae* and *Geomantia Nova*, in about 1140. As he either wrote or translated these books, Hugh of Santalla is sometimes credited with introducing geomancy to the West. Hugh was born in Santalla in northwest Spain, and worked as an alchemist, astrologer, and translator. He translated many works from the Arabic, including at least seven books on astrology and divination.

Other authors started writing books on geomancy, and also translated Islamic works into Latin and Hebrew. Plato of Tivoli, an Italian who lived in Barcelona from 1134 to 1145, translated many books on astrology and other subjects. Possibly his best known work was *Alfakini Arabici filii quaestiones geomantiae*, which became one of the standard works on geomancy.

Gerard of Cremona (c. 1114–87) is credited with translating the first book from the Arabic that utilized both geomancy and astrology to enable more information to be provided in the reading. All of these books describe the fundamentals of geomancy, but in later books the role of astrology gradually increased.

An example of this, dating back to 1262, was recorded by Rolandino da Padova, an Italian historian and academic:

> *For behold in those days, while your Highness* [Ezzelino da Romano] *was besieging Padua during your campaign, some of the prisoners anxiously used divination (sortes) to find out what would happen to*

your army. One of them, by means of special dots used in one technique which they call 'geomancy' (a word I haven't come across before), seemed to say that Padua would not be captured at this time, claiming—and I don't understand this—that the first house, relating to the army, seemed to be Lesser Fortune, while the figure of the seventh house, which represents "enemies," was Greater Fortune. [2]

It took another hundred years for geomancy to be mentioned in a book published in England. This was in an alliterative poem called *The Vision Concerning Piers the Plowman*, attributed to William Langland (c. 1330– c. 1400). This poem appeared in three versions between 1362 and 1399. William Langland was obviously not impressed with geomancy, as he wrote:

But astronomy is a hard thing and evil to know;
Geometry and geomancy are guileful of speech;
Who so works at these two must stay awake late,
For sorcery is the sovereign book of that science.

In about 1387, in *The Parson's Tale*, the twenty-third section of *The Canterbury Tales*, by Geoffrey Chaucer (c. 1343–1400), geomancy was also dismissed. ("What say we of them that believe in divynailes [divinations] as . . . geomancie . . .")

In *The Travels of Sir John Mandeville*, originally written in French in the late fourteenth century, geomancy was described as "that superstitious arte."

Despite these less than favorable views on the subject, geomancy continued to grow in popularity, and by the sixteenth century had become one of the most popular forms of divination in Europe and the Arab world. Henry Cornelius Agrippa, Christopher Cattan, and John Heydon were just a few of the many authorities who wrote books on the subject.

Henry Cornelius Agrippa (1486–1535) was the most influential of these, and his books are still being read and studied almost five hundred years after his death. Agrippa wrote *Of Geomancy*, which was included in the *Fourth Book of Occult Philosophy*, published in 1567. Most of the *Fourth Book* appears spurious, but *Of Geomancy* is apparently genuine and describes Agrippa's own method of geomancy. Occult scholar Donald Tyson wrote: "*Of Geomancy* seems to be genuine, if the style and content are any guide—it is completely in keeping with the tone and attitude Agrippa displays in the *Occult Philosophy*."[3]

Cornelius Agrippa developed his own system of astrological geomancy. The geomantic figures are created and placed into the twelve astrological houses in a specific order. In addition, Agrippa also used the planets that related to the different figures to enable a more comprehensive interpretation.

The next major figure in the history of geomancy was Christopher Cattan, an Italian astrologer and soldier, who published his 288-page book on geomancy in 1558. Francis Sperry translated the French edition of his book into English, and it was published in 1591 as *The Geomancie of Maister Christopher Cattan, Gentleman*. The subtitle reads: "A booke, no less pleasant and recreatiue, then of a wittie inuention to knowe all things, past, present, and to come."

Cattan's book proved extremely popular, and was reprinted in 1608. As the Catholic Church started including occult books in their indices of prohibited books in 1554, Cattan was careful to write that geomancy worked, not because of "diabolicke invocation, but a part of Natural Magicke, and daughter of Astrology . . . and S. Thomas of Aquine [St. Thomas Aquinas] himself, a doctor of the church of no small estimation, saith in his *Quolibet* that it [geomancy] may bee admitted, because it doth participate with Astrologie, and is called her Daughter."

Robert Fludd (1574–1637), the English physician, philosopher, astrologer, memory expert, and prolific author, must have read Christopher Cattan's book, as geomancy was one of his many interests. In his encyclopedia of philosophy, *Utriusque cosmi maioris scilicet et minoris metaphysica*, published between 1617 and 1619, Fludd included four books on geomancy (*De Geomantia*),[4] which included an interesting personal story.

While traveling in France in 1601 and 1602, Fludd was forced by bad weather to spend the winter in Avignon. One evening, while drinking after dinner, he had a lengthy discussion on astrological geomancy with a group of people who were staying at the same house as he was. Some of these people were opposed to the art, while others were convinced of its veracity. In the course of defending the art, Fludd's comments demonstrated that he was knowledgeable on the subject.

After the conversation, he returned to his room. A young man who had been at the table followed him, and asked him to help him with a problem he had. He was in love with a young lady and wanted to know if his love was reciprocated, and if she loved him more than anyone else. Robert Fludd made excuses, but eventually agreed to construct a chart.

After doing this, Fludd described the physical shape and attributes of the woman, even telling the young man about a wart she had on her left eyelid. He then said she loved vineyards. The young man was excited, and told Fludd that the girl's mother had built her home in a place surrounded by vineyards.

Fludd then told him the bad news. According to his chart, the young woman was unfaithful and loved someone else. The young man confessed that he had always thought this might be the case. He returned to his companions and told them about the geomantic reading.

Word spread about the reading, and two people told Carlo Conti di Poli, the Vice-Legate, that a foreigner was predicting the future with geomancy, a practice that was not approved by the Catholic Church. Fortunately, the Vice-Legate was not overly concerned. He told the people who'd complained to him that there was probably not a single cardinal in all Italy who had not had an astrological or geomantic chart drawn up and interpreted.

A few days later, the Vice-Legate invited Fludd for dinner to talk about geomancy. Fludd was understandably nervous and took a friend with him, in case he needed a witness. He was painfully aware that his geomantic reading could lead to him being interrogated by the Inquisition. Fortunately, the Vice-Legate was genuinely interested in the subject, and wanted to know how it worked. Fludd told him that geomancy came from the soul. Rays emanated from the mind into the soul of the world, and then returned with information about the future. The Vice-Legate asked many more questions, which Fludd answered with many references to the Bible and philosophy, to show that geomancy was a natural, rather than a supernatural, art.

Finally, the Vice-Legate produced paper and pen and quickly cast a geomantic chart, which he interpreted, demonstrating that he was also a master of the art of geomancy.[5]

There is a slight possibility that Napoleon Bonaparte used a form of geomancy that was described in *The Book of Fate*. This book enjoyed great success in the nineteenth century, probably because of its association with Napoleon. Herman Kirchenhoffer, the translator and probably author of this book, claimed the manuscript was found in an ancient tomb by a scholar who accompanied Napoleon when he invaded Egypt in 1801. According to the story, the manuscript was translated into French, and Napoleon used it regularly until he lost it in 1813 during the Battle of Leipzig. After Napoleon's death, this book became hugely popular in Britain, where it was frequently used as a parlor game. Young men consulted it to see if they would become rich. Single women also consulted it to see when they would meet their future husbands. Napoleon's *Book of Fate* is still available. I remember my grandmother using it when I was a small boy.

Even if Napoleon had no interest in the subject, geomancy was a popular form of divination in France in the eighteenth and nineteenth centuries. At the end of the eighteenth century, Mme. la Maréchale de Clérambault was one of Paris's best-known fortunetellers. Although her specialty was cartomancy (divination with playing cards), she became famous because of her ability to read the future "through the art of little dots."[6]

Francis Barrett, the mysterious occultist and author, mentioned geomancy in his influential book *The Magus*, published in 1801. Interestingly, John Parkin, a Lincolnshire cunning man (practitioner of folk magic and a natural healer), was a former student of Francis Barrett. He developed and used his own system of geomancy.

Eighty years later, it was his system that became part of the curriculum of the Hermetic Order of the Golden Dawn, the influential occult order that was established in March 1888.[7] Geomancy was taught in the second of the five grades that the Golden Dawn offered when it was first established. Additional grades were added in 1891. Although the Golden Dawn offered a simplified form of geomancy, it was enough to keep the art alive.

During the twentieth century, Israel Regardie, Stephen Skinner, and John Michael Greer wrote books on the subject, introducing many people to the gentle art of geomancy.

Geomancy, or "a different astrology than we know today,"[8] was mentioned in Dan Brown's best-selling novel *The Lost Symbol*. His book introduced millions of people to geomancy and created a whole new interest in the subject. It's possible that more people today than ever before are using geomancy to enrich and enhance their lives.

one

What Is Geomancy?

Geomancy is the art of divination that, traditionally, uses marks made on the earth. There are many geomantic methods, but by far the most popular method involves the use of sixteen geomantic figures, which are created after the geomancer makes a random series of marks. The figures created by this process are interpreted to answer the person's question. This is the form of geomancy that is the subject of this book.

Geomancy has another meaning, also. Geomancy can be described as living in harmony with the earth. The ancient art of feng shui deals exclusively with this form of geomancy.[1] This form of geomancy considers the earth to be sacred, and people risk unforeseen consequences when they tamper with it. In the past, people paid attention to the well-being of the earth, and deliberately tried to live in harmony with it by utilizing the cycles of the seasons, crop rotation, sources of water, and even the placement of fields and buildings. Sadly, few people today pay much attention to this, and we will ultimately pay a heavy price if we fail to look after our planet. Remnants of this form of geomancy still exist in protective ceremonies, such as the laying of foundation stones.

Creating the Figures

The geomancer starts by thinking of a question. Once the geomancer has this question firmly in mind, he or she constructs a geomantic figure. This is done by making lines of small vertical marks on the ground or on a sheet of paper. Each row of marks is made in a right-to-left order. Since the idea is to create a random number of marks, the geomancer—who should be in a relaxed state of mind—thinks of the question but otherwise pays little attention to the process, while making the marks as rapidly as possible. It takes four rows of marks to create a geomantic figure. After the geomancer has made four rows of marks, the number of marks in each row is counted. **An odd number of marks creates a single dot, and an even number creates two dots.** Here is an example:

$$
\begin{array}{lll}
\bigcirc & \text{(15 dots)} & \text{. . . . .} \\
\bigcirc\ \bigcirc & \text{(16 dots)} & \text{. . . . .} \\
\bigcirc\ \bigcirc & \text{(18 dots)} & \text{. . . . .} \\
\bigcirc\ \bigcirc & \text{(16 dots)} & \text{. . . . .}
\end{array}
$$

Gradually, the process of creating the figures became easier. Geomancers started making marks with pen on paper. During the Renaissance, it was possible to obtain geomantic dice that had either one or two marks on each face. Four dice were tossed to create a single figure. The British Museum has a thirteenth-century Islamic divination device made of metal that creates geomantic figures randomly.[2]

More than twenty years ago, my good friend Dusty Cravens made me a set of rune sticks, using ebony inlaid with holly. There are four sticks in the set, and they each contain one mark on one side of the stick and two on the other. You can buy rune sticks from New Age stores, but they are not hard to make. All you need are four oblong sticks about three to six inches long and one-half to three-quarters of an inch wide. On one side of each stick, paint a single straight line. On the other side, paint two straight lines parallel to each other. If you prefer, you might paint a single circle on one side and two circles on the other. In fact, the sticks can be any size. A friend of mine, the late Orville Meyer, a well-known psychic, had a miniature set of sticks that he carried in his shirt pocket. They were about an inch-and-a-half long.

You will also need a casting cloth. Again the size is not critical. My casting cloth is made of dark blue velvet and is 18 inches square. The four sticks are held loosely in one hand and mixed. They are very gently tossed as I move my hand from the front of the casting cloth to the back. This tossing is virtually a spreading out of the sticks. As soon as the sticks have been cast, the hand that cast them covers the sticks and smooths them out. The casting and smoothing of the sticks is almost a single movement. Once this has been done, the hand is raised to reveal the geomantic figure.

The process is straightforward, but it takes a little practice to enable the sticks to fall away from the hand while almost simultaneously covering them so they cannot be seen until the figure has been formed.

Another method is to draw a circle on the ground and toss a handful of coins or small stones into it from a few feet away. After each toss, count the number of coins or stones inside the circle and create your figure that way.

Israel Regardie (1907–85), the American occultist and author, suggested using a bowl full of pebbles.[3] You reach in and take out a handful, which are counted to see if you have taken an odd or even number. I have a glass bowl containing the stones that are used for the game of *Go*. They make an intriguing display, and are useful for geomantic purposes.

Regardie also suggested using a pair of dice. After each throw, you can count the numbers on top of each die to see if they are odd or even. Naturally, you can also toss a single die, and use the odd or even number that appears on top.

When I lived in Cornwall, I knew a lady who used a bowl of small gemstones. She made a ritual out of the process. She would close her eyes and stir the gemstones while thinking about her question. She would then take a handful of stones. These were counted in the usual way to see if she had taken an even or odd number of them. However, instead of returning the stones to the bowl, she laid them out in a line. She did this four times to create the geomantic figure, and the lines of stones made an attractive display. When she interpreted the figure, she would also interpret the gemstones.

Some people prefer the traditional method of making marks in sand or earth. To do this, you'll need a shallow box that is at least two feet square. Fill it with sand or dry earth. This needs to come from an inland site, as sand obtained from the seashore relates to the element of Water, and is not suitable. Geomancy relates to the element of Earth. You will also need a length of dowel to make the rows of dots in the sand. You can use a pencil or short piece of wood, but it is better to make a wand for this. The marks are made on the sand from right to left.

Anything you make or use for geomantic purposes should be as attractive as possible. Do not let anyone else touch them. As the geomancer, you need to cast the figures yourself, even when giving a reading for someone else.

The Geomantic Figures

Sixteen figures, shown on the next page, can be created from four lines of dots, as long as there are only two possible results for each line.

Here is an example: Let's assume the top row contains 17 marks, the second row 14, the third 17, and the bottom row 15. As an odd number of marks is indicated by a single dot in the geomantic figure, and an even number is indicated by two marks, we have created the following figure:

    ◯   (17 dots) . . . .

  ◯ ◯ (14 dots)   . . . .

    ◯   (17 dots) . . . .

    ◯   (15 dots) . . . .

O	O O	O	O O
O	O	O O	O O
O	O	O	O
O	O	O	O
Via, the way	Caput Draconis, the dragon's head	Puella, the girl	Fortuna Major, major fortune

O	O O	O	O O
O	O	O O	O O
O O	O O	O O	O O
O	O	O	O
Puer, the boy	Acquisitio, gain	Carcer, the prison	Tristitia, the sadness

O	O O	O	O O
O	O	O O	O O
O	O	O	O
O O	O O	O O	O O
Cauda Draconis, the dragon's tail	Conjunctio, the union	Amissio, the loss	Albus, the white

O	O O	O	O O
O	O	O O	O O
O O	O O	O O	O O
O O	O O	O O	O O
Fortuna Minor, minor fortune	Rubeus, the red	Laetitia, the joy	Populus, the people

It may seem hard to believe that it's possible to give complete, detailed readings using such simple figures. We'll discuss how divination works in the next chapter, and in chapter 3 we'll look at these symbols in much more detail.

How Does It Work?

The word *divination* comes from the word *divine*. Divination accepts the soul, or divine principle, inside every person. Because of this, divination is considered a divine art.

People have always wanted to know what the future has in store for them. Consequently, well before recorded history, people devised different methods of divination to help them gain a glimpse of the future, or at least gain a greater understanding of their present circumstances. The earliest practitioners of divination were shamans or medicine men, and some of their methods are still used today. Ancient man gazed into the heavens looking for signs and portents in the night sky. This ultimately became astrology, an art that is practiced by more people today than ever before. People were fascinated with their dreams and sought out people who could interpret them. In the Bible, Joseph interpreted the dreams of the Pharaoh. Dream interpretation is still popular today. People studied signs and omens, such as the patterns created by smoke rising from a fire or the flight of a flock of birds. The ancient Greeks visited the oracle at Delphi to receive answers to their questions. Shamans divined from the earth, and became the first geomancers.

Divination is not the same as fortunetelling. Fortune-telling is the art of telling people about their future. Divination is the art of looking at a given situation from a different point of view, enabling the person to discover and examine a number of outcomes that he or she might not have considered before. Divination is a way to discern the truth of a situation. Divination enhances people's intuition, enabling them to temporarily forget their conscious minds and flow with their feelings. This gives them access to new ideas and different ways of looking at their current situations.

Divination always involves a question. The person requesting the divination wants information that he or she cannot obtain in any other way. The question may be as simple as "What will my future be like?" Alternatively, and more usefully, it might be "What will happen if I do such-and-such?" Divination questions can also involve the past. In medieval times, geomancers were kept busy with such questions as "Who stole our pig?" or "Where did I mislay my ring?" Before the telephone was invented, people would ask, "Is so-and-so at home?"

Most questions relate to people's personal concerns, such as love, money, health, and family. However, there is no limit to the type of questions that can be asked. Throughout history, geomancers, and other diviners, have been asked to answer questions on such topics as religion, politics, and the weather.

General questions receive generalized answers. Specific questions receive more detailed answers. However, as the answer comes in the form of symbols, highly specific questions create opportunities for misinterpretation. Divination will uncover the underlying truth of the situation, but may not provide every single detail.

Divination speaks in symbols that stimulate your intuition and imagination, enabling you to discover the hidden truths behind any given situation.

Throughout history, there have been many people who were able to divine the future with incredible accuracy. One of the most famous of these was Nostradamus. One of his lesser prophecies concerned the fate of two farm animals. Seigneur de Florinville, Nostradamus's landlord, asked him what would happen to the two piglets that lived in the farmyard. Nostradamus thought for a moment, and then said that a wolf would eat the white piglet, and that he and his landlord would eat the black one.

Seigneur de Florinville decided to play a trick on the famous seer, and asked his cook to kill the white piglet and prepare it for dinner that evening. The cook killed the white piglet and placed it on the kitchen table to prepare it for the oven. While his back was turned, a young wolf cub, who was kept in the house as a pet, dragged the carcass to the floor and started eating it. The cook knew nothing of the proposed trick, and immediately killed the black pig, cooked it, and served it to the two men that evening. As they ate the pig, de Florinville laughingly told Nostradamus that his prediction was wrong, as they were eating the white pig. Nostradamus insisted they were eating the black pig. His landlord sent for the cook, who told them what had occurred, and the previously skeptical de Florinville was forced to revise his opinion of his boarder's abilities.

Nostradamus was a remarkable man by any standards, and his prophecies are still being studied today. It's unlikely that you and I will ever be able to divine the future as well as he could. Fortunately, geomancy is a structured system of divination, and it's not necessary to have the skills of Nostradamus to provide helpful and accurate readings from it.

Different theories have been proposed as to how geomancy works. One theory says that as geomancy was originally performed by making marks in the earth, elemental spirits guide the hands of the person doing the divination, and ensure that he or she makes the correct number of marks.

Carl Jung thought about divination at great length, and came up with a theory of synchronicity. In his foreword to Richard Wilhelm's translation of the *I Ching*, Jung wrote: "It is assumed that the fall of the coins . . . is what it necessarily must be in a given 'situation,' inasmuch as anything happening in that moment belongs to it as an indispensable part of the picture."[1]

In other words, the way the coins land is the only possible result that could occur if the coins were tossed at that particular moment in time. If we relate this to geomancy, the figures created by dots on the ground, or any other method, are the only possible figures that could be created at that exact moment.

Unfortunately, it's not possible to prove or disprove these theories. Consequently, the only way to determine the validity of geomancy, or any other form of divination, is to test it. Take your time. Most people find it better to experiment with simpler methods before moving on to astrological geomancy.

Frequently, I find that the most useful information comes not from the divination itself, but from the fresh point of view the divination provides. Suppose, for example, that I'm performing a divination to assess a business opportunity. In the shield method, one of the most popular methods of geomancy, three figures are the most important. Suppose one of those figures is Puella, the girl. This denotes a female influence that I might not have become aware of in any other way. Now that I know this, I can act accordingly. This is an additional benefit to performing divinations.

Divination is not infallible. However, in my experience, it always provides information that is useful and relevant to the situation.

Geomancy is intended for serious questions, and shouldn't be used frivolously or for idle amusement. The same question should not be asked repeatedly, in the hope of obtaining a different outcome. You should also be in a peaceful, relaxed state of mind when performing the divination. Cornelius Agrippa wrote that geomancy should not be practiced "on a cloudy or rainy day, or when the weather is stormy, nor while the mind is disturbed by anger or oppressed with cares." I would agree to perform a divination on a cloudy or rainy day, but I would delay it if the weather were stormy. I would also never perform a divination if I felt angry or frustrated.

As long as you ask your questions seriously, and as completely as possible, you will receive accurate and insightful information.

You have already met the sixteen figures in geomancy. We'll discuss them in much more depth in the next chapter.

three

The Sixteen Symbols

The sixteen geomantic figures, illustrated on page 18, were given Latin names in medieval times. The figures are still known by these names today. These figures have also been related to the seven visible planets, the twelve signs of the zodiac, the four elements, the twelve months of the year, the seven days of the week, parts of the body, and different body types. The body type refers to the appearance of the person indicated by the particular figure. If, for instance, Puer appeared as one of the final figures in the divination, you would know that someone who was short and solidly built would be involved in the divination.

Puer—the Boy

Element: Fire

Zodiac sign: Aries

Planet: Mars

Month: March

Day: Monday

Parts of the body: Head, arms, shoulders

Body type: Short, solid build that is often muscular; small
eyes and uneven teeth

Puer is created by two odd-numbered lines above an
even line, with another odd line at the bottom. This creates
a figure that looks like a circle with a line above it. This is
similar to the symbol of a male (a circle with an arrow on
top pointing northeast).

Puer is associated with Mars, Fire, and the sign of Aries.
It relates to the traditional male attributes of physical activity, leadership, initiative, and responsibility. Nowadays, some
people dislike the idea of male and female activities being
defined in such a rigid way. However, thousands of years ago,
when geomancy was first established, this was a natural way
of looking at the sexes and their roles in everyday life.

Puer is a mixed figure. It is largely positive, but can
also be negative, as it indicates rashness and impulsiveness.
Traditionally, it was considered to be positive in war and
love, but negative in everything else. It usually represents a
young man who possesses a great deal of ability that needs
to be harnessed and used correctly. The important lesson of
Puer is to think before acting. When this figure is used posi-

tively, it's a sign of enthusiasm, competitiveness, initiative, courage, leadership ability, and the potential to achieve virtually anything.

Amissio—the Loss

Element: Earth

Zodiac sign: Taurus

Planet: Venus

Month: September

Day: Friday

Parts of the body: Kidneys, thighs, shoulders

Body type: Medium height and build; broad shoulders, long neck, and round face; small mouth and large eyes

Amissio is comprised of a single odd-numbered row on the top. Below this are an even row, an odd row, and another even row. These look like two upside-down bowls that relate to loss, illness, financial problems, and other difficulties.

Amissio relates to Venus, Earth, and the sign of Taurus. Despite its relationship to Venus, Amissio is a negative figure, as the word means "loss." This loss is usually money, but it can be anything, including the loss of love. It indicates a negative outcome to whatever the person is involved in. It is a strong warning for the person to be absolutely certain that everything he or she does is in the best interests of everyone concerned. If this person tries to take advantage of others, it will invariably end in failure. However, Amissio can also be a positive figure, if loss is the desired outcome. If someone wanted to lose weight, for instance, Amissio would be considered a positive figure.

Interestingly, this figure is traditionally associated with generosity and shows the person should remain generous, even if suffering loss himself or herself.

Albus—the White

Element: Air

Zodiac sign: Gemini

Planet: Mercury

```
O O
O O
  O
O O
```

Month: June

Day: Wednesday

Parts of the body: Shoulders, arms, eyes

Body type: Mesomorph (wide shoulders, narrow waist), medium height, large head

Albus is made up of two even-numbered rows above an odd-numbered row and another even-numbered row. With a little imagination, this looks like a full wine glass, which is fitting, as Albus signifies wisdom, peace, moderation, and consideration of others. Since *albus* means "white," another mnemonic might be to visualize Albus as a white-haired, wise old man drinking white wine.

Albus is related to Mercury, Air, and the sign of Gemini. It is a moderately fortunate figure, but it is not as positive as Conjunctio, the other figure governed by Mercury. Albus also indicates contemplation, spiritual growth, and the ability to balance all areas of life: physical, mental, and spiritual. Albus indicates slow but steady progress.

Populus—the People

Element: Water

Zodiac sign: Cancer

Planet: Moon

Month: December

Day: Monday

Part of the body: Abdomen

Body type: Ectomorph (tall, thin, long muscles), long face with prominent teeth

Populus is comprised of four even-numbered rows. These dots indicate people standing beside each other. Consequently, Populus represents friends, family, and group involvement.

Populus is related to the Moon, Water, and the sign of Cancer.

The word *populus* means "people," and represents a gathering of people. It is a neutral figure that, much like a crowd, reflects its surroundings. If good, positive thoughts are sent out, the results will be excellent. However, if negative thoughts or feelings are sent out, the results will affect the person negatively. It shows that the person has to learn from experience, and the future depends entirely on his or her approach to every situation. Ultimately, the outcome may not be entirely in his or her hands, as it may depend on the actions of others. Populus can also mean family, friends, and important news.

Fortuna Major—Major Fortune

Element: Fire

Zodiac sign: Leo

Planet: Sun

O O
O O
O
O

Month: January

Day: Sunday

Parts of the body: Throat, neck

Body type: Medium height, slim, open face with expressive eyes

Fortuna Major is formed by two rows of even numbers above two rows of odd numbers. My mnemonic is to view the two even rows as the heavens, and the two single rows as good fortune and success coming down from above.

Fortuna Major is an extremely positive figure, as it indicates great success, good luck, and protection. It has a strong connection with karma, as it shows that the good the person has done in the past enables him or her to enjoy good luck, success, happiness, and peace of mind in the future. It shows the person has sufficient inner strength to overcome any problem or difficulty. Fortuna Major also relates to property and possessions. The person will always be generous with his or her wealth. This figure shows that the person is liked and held in high esteem by others.

Conjunctio—the Union

Element: Earth

Zodiac sign: Virgo

Planet: Mercury

Month: August

Day: Wednesday

Parts of the body: Chest, nervous system

Body type: Medium height, graceful and slender build; long face with a mouth that curves upward

Conjunctio is made up of an even-numbered row at the top. Below this are two odd-numbered rows, with another even-numbered row at the bottom. This formation can be viewed as a cross or a kiss, symbolizing two people joined together.

Conjunctio is a highly fortunate figure that indicates a combining, or joining together. This relates to all types of relationships and includes friendship, love, and partnership. It even enables opposites to join together. It includes reunions, both of people and also the type of reunion that occurs when someone finds something that has been lost. Conjunctio shows that the person will have to use prudence and caution. He or she will need to think carefully, and decide exactly what he or she wants, before moving forward. This person will have to use logic as well as his or her emotions. He or she will also have to ensure that the union is beneficial to both parties. Conjunctio is beneficial for all matters involving contact with others, but is unfavorable for solitary activities.

Puella—the Girl

Element: Air

Zodiac sign: Libra

Planet: Venus

Month: September

Day: Wednesday

Parts of the body: Face, arms, feet, breasts

Body type: Medium height, tendency to be overweight; round face with small mouth, prominent shoulders

Puella is formed by an odd number at the top, followed by an even number, with two odd numbers below. I have a mnemonic to help me remember this. Puella looks vaguely like a circle with a line below it, and this is similar to the symbol for a female (a circle with a plus sign beneath it).

As *puella* means "young girl," this figure relates to women, and the traditional feminine qualities of birth, healing, nurturing, intuition, and wisdom. It is an indication of pleasant dealings with women and is a positive sign for family relationships, as it promises harmony and happiness. For a man, this figure relates to his relationship with his wife and daughters. For a woman, Puella relates to harmonious relationships with the other women in her family: mother, mother-in-law, and daughters.

Puella is usually, but not always, a positive figure. An attractive woman is not always a good person. Puella can be fickle, superficial, and indecisive. Puella is most useful when the person's question relates to love and close relationships. It promises happiness in the immediate future. However, it is not as positive if the question relates to long-term happiness.

Rubeus—the Red

Element: Water

Zodiac sign: Scorpio

Planet: Mars

Month: March

Day: Tuesday

Part of the body: Chest

Body type: Medium height, muscular body, reddish skin, and ruddy complexion

Rubeus is made up of an even-numbered row, above an odd-numbered row and two even-numbered rows. This looks like an upside-down wine glass, representing emptiness.

Rubeus is ruled by Mars, Water, and the sign of Scorpio. As *rubeus* means "red," this figure indicates violence, danger, passion, and temper. Rubeus is a challenging, and usually unfavorable, figure that frequently leaves upheaval, disruption, and anger in its wake. It shows that the person needs to take time out to think matters through, and to decide how to move forward again. While licking his or her wounds, this person will gradually become aware that the problems being faced were most probably self-inflicted. As long as this person is prepared to listen to his or her inner voice, the right path for the future will ultimately be found.

Acquisitio—Gain

Element: Fire

Zodiac sign: Sagittarius

Planet: Jupiter

Month: March

Day: Thursday

Parts of the body: Hips and thighs

Body type: Short, well-built, short neck, large head, and round face

Acquisitio has an even row of numbers on top. Below this are an odd-numbered row, an even row, and another odd-numbered row. This looks similar to two bowls facing upwards. That happens to be my mnemonic for this figure, as I imagine the bowls to be full (gain).

Acquisitio is a successful figure that relates to Jupiter, Sagittarius, and the element of Fire. The word *acquisitio* means "acquiring," and this usually relates to possessions and financial reward. It represents gain, profit, and worldly success. It shows that all the hard work and problems from the past are now behind the person, who has learned from past failures and is now moving forward. The person will enjoy the rewards of success, and will, one hopes, spend some time developing spiritually and intuitively.

Carcer—the Prison

Element: Earth

Zodiac sign: Capricorn

Planet: Saturn

Month: February

Day: Saturday

Parts of the body: Bones, stomach, bladder, feet

Body type: Medium height, wiry build, long neck, small eyes

Carcer is created by an odd-numbered row at the top. Beneath this are two even-numbered rows, and another odd-numbered row at the bottom. This looks like two bowls pressed together, confining whatever is inside them.

Carcer relates to Saturn, Earth, and the sign of Capricorn. As the word *carcer* means "prison," this figure is a sign of limitations, restrictions, isolation, and confinement. It also indicates obstacles, delays, worries, and indecision. Carcer can be a favorable figure if the question concerns stability and security.

Carcer warns that the person needs to pay close attention to his or her emotions—especially anger, greed, and jealousy. As Carcer can also mean delays and obstacles, this person needs to accept the situation as it is, work productively, and wait patiently until the period of negativity is over. Carcer is often a learning experience. When Carcer is the Judge (see chapter 4), the person asking the question will receive what he or she has earned.

Tristitia—the Sadness

Element: Air

Zodiac sign: Aquarius

Planet: Saturn

Month: October

Day: Saturday

Parts of the body: Kidneys, liver

Body type: Tall, thin, prominent joints, and large feet; long, thin face and prominent teeth

Tristitia is created by three even rows above a single odd-numbered row. This looks like an upside-down rainbow, and is a sign of loneliness, disappointment, unhappiness, and possibly depression.

The word *tristitia* means "melancholy." It indicates grief, sadness, and the possibility of a major loss. This is likely to happen without warning, and the person will have to cope with the destruction or loss of something that has been carefully built up. The likely response to this is for the person to blame everyone else for the situation. However, the lesson is for the person to learn from the experience and become more charitable, forgiving, and unselfish.

Laetitia—the Joy

O

O O

O O

O O

Element: Water

Zodiac sign: Pisces

Planet: Jupiter

Month: April

Day: Thursday

Part of the body: Solar plexus

Body type: Tall, muscular, athletic build; prominent forehead

Laetitia is made up of an odd-numbered row on top of three even-numbered rows. This looks like a rainbow, which is appropriate as this is the most fortunate figure of all. It indicates joy, happiness, good fortune, contentment, and peace of mind.

Laetitia is related to Jupiter, Water, and the sign of Pisces.

Laetitia also indicates creativity, good health, and future happiness. It gives the person a positive approach to life and an abundance of energy. This person has usually achieved his or her major goals and has gained knowledge and wisdom that he or she is willing to share with others. It indicates a balance between the spiritual and material sides of the person's nature, and shows that he or she is living in harmony with the universe and is continuing to make forward progress.

Cauda Draconis—the Dragon's Tail

Element: Fire

○

Zodiac sign: Sagittarius

○

○

Planet: South Node
of the Moon

○ ○

Month: November

Day: Saturday

Parts of the body: Male genitals, feet

Body type: Tall, thin, with long toes and fingers; long face
with large nose

Cauda Draconis is made up of three odd-numbered rows above an even-numbered row. With a little imagination, this looks something like a dragon's tail.

Cauda Draconis relates to the South Node of the Moon and indicates where the Moon crosses the path of the Sun heading south. As it is descending in this placement, it has always been considered a negative figure that relates to disruption, endings, bad luck, sudden losses, and ill fortune. It shows that the person must be prepared to walk away from the past and start life anew. There will be a great deal of hurt and bitterness, and the person will have to learn to let go and learn from the experience. This person will also have to accept that he or she is reaping the rewards of past actions. Although Cauda Draconis signifies endings, it also promises a new beginning. Consequently, although it is usually an unfavorable figure, it is favorable for anything that is nearing its natural end.

When Cauda Draconis appears in the first house (see chapter 5), many geomancers destroy the chart and refuse to answer the question.

Caput Draconis—the Dragon's Head

Element: Earth

Zodiac sign: Virgo

Planets: Venus and Jupiter

Month: August

Day: Saturday

Parts of the body: Female sexual organs, liver

Body type: Medium height, light build, pleasant face

Caput Draconis is created from a line containing an even number of dots above three lines containing an odd number of dots. My mnemonic for remembering this is that this combination can be pictured as the eyes and snout of the dragon's head.

Caput Draconis represents the Moon's North Node. The nodes indicate the two positions when the Moon crosses the ecliptic. The North Node occurs when, because of the tilt of the earth's axis, the Moon appears to move from the southern hemisphere to the northern hemisphere. This is often called the *dragon's head*, as whenever an eclipse occurs, the dragon Moon appears to swallow the Sun.

Caput Draconis is a positive figure, as it indicates birth, innocence, new starts, beginnings, and boundless opportunities. However, it is an interesting figure, as it becomes more positive when surrounded by other positive figures, but less positive when surrounded by negative figures. It usually indicates an improvement in the person's circumstances, sometimes after a difficult start. Caput Draconis also indicates the person will help others but will remain aware of his or her own needs at the same time. Because of this, it also indicates shrewdness and alertness. The person will have complete faith in whatever it is he or she is doing.

Fortuna Minor—the Minor Fortune

Element: Fire

Zodiac sign: Leo

Planet: Sun

Month: April

Day: Sunday

Parts of the body: Head, brain

Body type: Medium height, heavy build, large nose, thick hair

Fortuna Minor is made up of two odd-numbered rows above two even rows. The even rows can be imagined as the earth, and the two odd rows can represent good luck coming from the earth.

Fortuna Minor, like Fortuna Major, is related to Fire, Leo, and the Sun. However, Fortuna Major is related to the Sun during the day, while Fortuna Minor symbolizes the Sun at night. (Although it can't be seen at night, the Sun is, of course, still there.) Consequently, it is a sign of lesser success. Despite this, it shows that the person is protected from adversity and misfortune, and will gradually learn and grow from every experience until he or she achieves success. This person must be prepared to work hard when necessary, but also be prepared to slow down, relax, meditate, and get in touch with his or her inner self from time to time. Although it may not happen quickly, Fortuna Minor indicates ultimate success, power, possessions, and influence. Often, this success is obtained with outside help, rather than solely by the person's own skill, talent, and hard work.

Via—the Way

Element: Water

Zodiac sign: Cancer

Planet: Moon

Month: July

Day: Monday

Part of the body: Stomach

Body type: Endomorph (pear-shaped), medium height, tendency to be overweight

Via is created by four odd numbers, creating a single line of dots that form a road or a path. In fact, I visualize this row of dots as a road, and this acts as a mnemonic to help me remember the meaning of this figure.

The Latin word *via* means "street" or "way." This indicates a journey, or a forward action of some sort. It can also represent the opening of a doorway, such as being exposed to new ideas. It can also indicate time spent alone. Consequently, it can sometimes be a lonely figure. The presence of Via shows that the person has either found the right direction and knows where he or she is going, or is searching for the right direction. Via relates to change and is a highly positive figure if change is desired. However, it is less favorable if the person prefers the status quo and does not want to change.

As Via is related to the Moon, the Water element, and the sign of Cancer, the person will possess a great deal of empathy, understanding, and tact. Because of these qualities, the person will achieve his or her goal smoothly and without antagonizing others.

How to Perform a Quick Divination

Now that you know the basic meanings of the sixteen figures, you can use them to answer questions. Be as specific as you can when asking your question. You need to create the figure while concentrating on your question.

Let's assume you ask, "Will I receive my promised pay raise next month?" While thinking of this question, you need to produce four rows of dots on a sheet of paper. Make a series of dots, using a pen or pencil, starting at the right-hand side of the sheet of paper and stopping sometime before reaching the left-hand side of the paper. Do this four times to generate four rows of dots. Once you have done this, add up the number of dots in each row. An odd number of dots indicate a single mark, and an even number of dots indicates two marks. If, for instance, your four rows of dots total 15, 16, 18, and 14, you will have generated the figure known as Laetitia, which is created by one single lines above three double lines.

The outcome will be positive if the figure you create is Laetitia, Fortuna Major, Fortuna Minor, or Acquisitio. However, it is probably unlikely that you'll receive the raise if you create Amissio, Cauda Draconis, Tristitia, or Carcer.

The two figures that represent boy and girl are not quite as easy to interpret. If you create Puer, your raise could well occur if you demonstrate enthusiasm and initiative. Puella indicates short-term success and happiness. This tends to indicate that you'll receive the raise, but may also receive additional responsibilities or tasks to perform.

Caput Draconis indicates financial advancement through a new beginning. This may well indicate that you take on a new role at the same time as you receive your pay raise.

Conjunctio is the figure of unions. Your raise may depend on how well you get along with other people at your workplace. As this is a figure of temperance, the raise might not be as large as you expected.

The presence of Rubeus is a strong indication that you need to keep your emotions in check to receive the pay raise. Any emotional outbursts would severely hinder your chances.

Albus is a favorable figure that indicates slow, steady progress. This means you'll probably get your raise, but it might not be as large as you wish. It will probably be one of many small raises you'll receive during the course of your career.

Here is another question: "What will my future husband look like?" To answer this, all you need do is generate a figure, and see what body type relates to it. If you created Caput Draconis, for instance, your future husband will be of medium height and have a slight build. He will also have a pleasant face.

Simple questions can be answered by creating a single figure. It's also a good way to practice and to learn the meanings of each figure. However, for most questions, it's better to create a chart. We'll start doing that in the next chapter when we meet the Mothers, Daughters, Nieces, Witnesses, and Judge, all of whom play an important role in geomancy.

four

Meet the Family

It's possible to give helpful readings by creating a single figure, but this is not likely to provide enough information if a more specific and comprehensive answer is required. Consequently, over the centuries, a variety of methods have been devised to enable fuller, more detailed answers.

The best known of these is called the shield (chart 4A), as the figures are placed on a grid that looks like a shield. The starting point is to think of your question, and to continue thinking about it while you cast four figures.

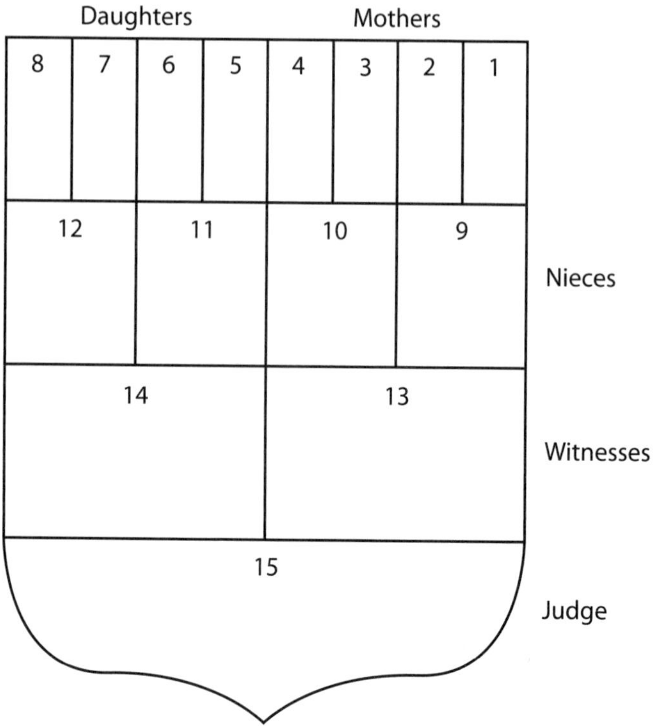

Chart 4A: Traditional geomantic chart (the shield)

The Four Mothers

The first four figures are called the Mothers, as they give birth to all the other figures. The four Mothers are placed in the four spaces at the top right-hand side of the shield. The first Mother dealt is placed on the outside, far right position, and the others follow in right-to-left order.

It is not necessary to cast any more figures, as the other figures are all derived from the Mothers. The first of these are the four Daughters.

To create the four Daughters, it's necessary to look at the Mothers in a different way. The figures are created from four rows of dots. The top, or uppermost, dot can be considered the Mother's head, while the second dot, or dots, are called the neck. The third dot, or dots, from the top are called the body, and the bottom dot, or dots, are called the feet. We need this information to create the four Daughters.

$$\begin{array}{ll} \bigcirc & \text{Head} \\ \bigcirc\ \bigcirc & \text{Neck} \\ \bigcirc\ \bigcirc & \text{Body} \\ \bigcirc\ \bigcirc & \text{Feet} \end{array}$$

The Four Daughters

The Daughters are created by rearranging the four figures that make up the Mothers. The first Daughter is created from the heads of the four Mothers. The head of the first Mother becomes the head of the first Daughter. The head of the second Mother becomes the neck of the first Daughter. The head of the third Mother becomes the body of the first Daughter. Finally, the head of the fourth Mother becomes the feet of the first Daughter.

The second Daughter is created in exactly the same way, but this time the necks of the four Mothers are used to create the figure of the second Daughter. The third Daughter is created from the bodies of the four Mothers, and the fourth Daughter is derived from the Mothers' feet.

The four Daughters are placed in the shield next to the Mothers. The first Daughter is placed beside the fourth Mother, and the others are placed in order from right to left.

The Four Nieces

The next figures to be created are the four Nieces. (The Hermetic Order of the Golden Dawn called these figures the four Nephews, which is why many recent books call them by this name.) The Nieces are created from both the Mothers and the Daughters.

The first Niece is created from the first and second Mothers. The head of the first Niece is formed by adding up the number of dots in the heads of the first and second Mothers. If the total is an odd number (which occurs when one Mother has one dot and the other two dots), the first Niece will have one dot as her head. If the total is an even number, she will have two dots in this position.

The neck, body, and feet of the first Niece are created in the same way.

The second Niece is formed using the third and fourth Mothers. The third Niece is created from the first and second Daughters, and the fourth Niece is created from the third and fourth Daughters.

Here's an example. Let's assume we're creating a Niece from Laetitia and Albus. This creates Amissio:

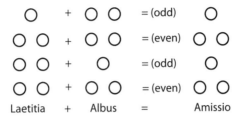

Laetitia	+	Albus	=	Amissio

The Two Witnesses

The two Witnesses are created in exactly the same way as the Nieces. The first Witness is created from the first and second Nieces, and is placed in the right-hand position on the shield. The second Witness is created from the third and fourth Nieces and is placed on the left-hand side of the shield.

The Judge

There is one position left on the shield: the bottom center. This place is reserved for the Judge. He is created in the same way as the Nieces and the Witnesses. The two Witnesses are added together, and this creates the Judge.

Example

Let's assume you have formulated a question and have cast sixteen rows of dots to create the four Mothers. These are:

	First Mother	Second Mother
Head	O O	O
Neck	O	O O
Body	O	O O
Feet	O	O
	Caput Draconis	Carcer

	Third Mother	Fourth Mother
Head	O	O O
Neck	O	O
Body	O O	O
Feet	O O	O O
	Fortuna Minor	Conjunctio

Creating the Daughters

The first Daughter is created from the heads of each Mother:

OO + O + O + OO

O O
O
O
O O

Conjunctio

The second Daughter is created from the necks of each Mother:

O + OO + O + O

O

O O

O

O

Puella

The third Daughter is created from the bodies of each Mother:

O + OO + OO + O

O

O O

O O

O

Carcer

The fourth Daughter is created from the feet of each Mother:

O + O + OO + OO

O

O

O O

O O

Fortuna Minor

Creating the Nieces

The first Niece is created from the first and second Mothers:

First Mother		Second Mother		First Niece
O O	+	O	= (odd)	O
O	+	O O	= (odd)	O
O	+	O O	= (odd)	O
O	+	O	= (even)	O O

The second Niece is created from the third and fourth Mothers:

Third Mother		Fourth Mother		Second Niece
O	+	O O	= (odd)	O
O	+	O	= (even)	O O
O O	+	O	= (odd)	O
O O	+	O O	= (even)	O O

The third Niece is created from the first and second Daughters:

First Daughter		Second Daughter		Third Niece
O O	+	O	= (odd)	O
O	+	O O	= (odd)	O
O	+	O	= (even)	O O
O O	+	O	= (odd)	O

The fourth Niece is created from the third and fourth Daughters:

Third Daughter	Fourth Daughter		Fourth Niece
O	+ O	= (even)	O O
O O	+ O	= (odd)	O
O O	+ O O	= (even)	O O
O	+ O O	= (odd)	O

Creating the Witnesses

The Witnesses are created in exactly the same way. The Right Witness (the Witness on the right-hand side of the shield) is created from the first and second Nieces:

First Niece	Second Niece		Right Witness
O	+ O	= (even)	O O
O	+ O O	= (odd)	O
O	+ O	= (even)	O O
O O	+ O O	= (even)	O O

The Left Witness is created from the third and fourth Nieces:

Third Niece	Fourth Niece		Left Witness
O	+ O O	= (odd)	O
O	+ O	= (even)	O O
O O	+ O O	= (even)	O O
O	+ O	= (even)	O O

Creating the Judge

The final figure to be created is the Judge. This is formed from the two Witnesses:

Right Witness		Left Witness	Judge
O O	+	O	= (odd)	O
O	+	O O	= (odd)	O
O O	+	O O	= (even)	O O
O O	+	O O	= (even)	O O

In this example, the Judge is Fortuna Minor. Interestingly, only eight of the sixteen figures can ever be the Judge. This is because the Mothers and Daughters are created from the same dots that have been moved around to create a different arrangement. As the Judge is the only figure created from both sides of the shield, the figures that represent him must always have an even number of dots. Consequently, the only figures that can ever represent the Judge are: Acquisitio, Amissio, Carcer, Conjunctio, Fortuna Major, Fortuna Minor, Populus, and Via. It's a sign that something has gone wrong in your calculations if you produce a different figure. This can be a useful check to ensure your calculations are correct.

We have now created our first chart. The next step is to interpret it, and find out what it all means.

How to Interpret the Chart

As you have seen, constructing the chart is basically mathematical. However, once it has been created the process becomes more interesting, creative, and intuitive. When you interpret the chart, you'll use some of the figures that have been created to weave a story that will answer the person's question.

If the question is a simple one that can be answered by "yes" or "no," all you need do is examine the Judge and determine if it is favorable or unfavorable.

If you need more detail, you can examine the two Witnesses. The Right Witness represents the person asking the question. It also represents this person's past. (The Judge represents the present, and the Left Witness indicates the future.) The Left Witness also represents the outside circumstances relating to the question.

The Witnesses have another important part to play in the reading. If the Judge is a favorable figure that has been created from two favorable Witnesses, the outcome will be extremely favorable. Likewise, if the Judge is an unfavorable figure, created from two unfavorable Witnesses, the outcome will be even worse than the indication provided by the Judge alone. If the Judge and Witnesses comprise a mixture of favorable and unfavorable figures, the outcome will be mixed.

In the example on the previous page, the Judge is Fortuna Minor, which denotes a favorable outcome. The Witnesses are Rubeus (Right Witness) and Laetitia (Left Witness). Laetitia is extremely favorable, but Rubeus is usually unfavorable. Consequently, if we had looked solely at the Judge, we would have looked forward to a positive outcome to our question. However, a negative and a positive Witness modify this interpretation.

The actual reading depends on the question that has been asked. Let's imagine that the person asking the question is a young man who has fallen in love with a young woman, and wants to know if the relationship will last. In this instance, we might say:

"The Judge is Fortuna Minor, which is usually a positive sign. It indicates success and a possibly short-lived gain. Unfortunately, it's not a good indication for a relationship that is intended to be long-term. Consequently, we need to look at the two Witnesses to see how they modify this. The right-hand Witness is the more important one, as it also represents you. Rubeus is a passionate, hot-headed, sometimes emotional figure. Because of this, you are likely to lose your temper easily, overreact to small things, and even lash out if the situation becomes difficult. Because of all this, Rubeus is usually considered a negative figure, and shows that you need to concentrate on remaining calm and relaxed, no matter what provocation you receive. This will prove difficult for you, but if you don't overcome it, you'll have major problems, not just with this relationship, but in all areas of your life. Keep your feet on the ground, think before you act, and don't do anything hastily or in the heat of the moment.

"The Left Witness is also important, as it reveals the future. Here you have Laetitia, one of the most positive figures it's possible to have. It indicates joy, happiness, and forward progress. Consequently, if you manage to control your negative feelings (Rubeus) and capitalize on the immediate success indicated by the Judge (Fortuna Minor), you have the potential for great happiness and success in the future. The future may prove extremely positive, as long as you treat your partner fairly and behave like a mature adult."

If the person needs further information, it's possible to cast another figure, known as a Reconciler, by combining the first Mother and the Judge. In this instance it creates:

First Mother			Judge		Reconciler
O O	+		O	=	O
O	+		O	=	O O
O	+		O O	=	O
O	+		O O	=	O

The figure created by this combination is Puella. This is a positive figure to receive in any divination concerning love and friendship. However, Puella can be fickle, and it sometimes indicates happiness in short-term relationships.

As the Judge also indicates short-term success, our young man will have to think carefully before proceeding. However, this particular Reconciler is a good one to receive to help answer this question. Our young friend will need to look at himself carefully (Rubeus), and work hard on improving himself, if he wants the relationship to be a permanent, long-lasting one.

More information can be found by examining the four Mothers. In this example we have Caput Draconis, Carcer, Fortuna Minor, and Conjunctio.

Caput Draconis, the first Mother, is a positive figure here, as it indicates new beginnings. However, as it can be extremely positive in some circumstances and less so in others, we need to look at the other Mothers.

Carcer, the second Mother, is usually considered to be negative. However, it can be favorable if the question involves stability and security. In this reading, it most probably indicates delays.

The third Mother is Fortuna Minor. This confirms the interpretation given for the Judge, who also happens to be Fortuna Minor.

The fourth Mother is extremely important, as she relates to the final outcome of the question. In this position we have Conjunctio. This is a positive figure for relationships and indicates the couple will be happy. This is further confirmation that the relationship will be a lasting one.

Here is another example. Let's assume you've been unwell for some time, and your question is: "Will I recover from my illness?" Usually, you would also ask if you'd recover within a certain period of time, but as you've been ill for some time, all you want to know now is if you will ever recover.

Here are the figures you created to answer this question:

First Mother	Second Mother	Third Mother	Fourth Mother
O O	O	O	O O
O O	O O	O	O
O	O O	O	O
O	O	O	O
Fortuna Major	Carcer	Via	Caput Draconis

First Daughter	Second Daughter	Third Daughter	Fourth Daughter
O O	O O	O	O
O	O O	O O	O
O	O	O	O
O O	O	O	O
Conjunctio	Fortuna Major	Puella	Via

First Niece

○

○ ○

○

○ ○

Amissio

Second Niece

○

○ ○

○ ○

○ ○

Leatitia

Third Niece

○ ○

○

○ ○

○

Acquisitio

Fourth Niece

○ ○

○

○ ○

○ ○

Rubus

Left Witness

○ ○

○ ○

○ ○

○

Tristitia

Right Witness

○ ○

○ ○

○

○ ○

Albus

Judge

○ ○

○ ○

○

○

Fortuna Major

You can immediately see that the Judge is highly favorable, and indicates that you will recover. The Right Witness, Albus, indicates peacefulness and insight. It also shows that you might need help from others. The Left Witness, Tristitia, indicates a loss in the future. This could well indicate the loss of your illness. Tristitia is usually a negative figure that could indicate illness, but coupled with Albus and Fortuna Major, it indicates a complete recovery. There is no need to create a Reconciler, as the Witnesses and Judge provide a complete answer to the question.

As you can see, with just a little practice, you'll be able to work out the meanings of the Witnesses and Judge without referring to the previous chapter. However, while you're learning, you might find it helpful to refer to a list that gives brief answers to every possible combination of Witnesses and Judges. You should not rely solely on these answers. Frequently, a Reconciler is required to provide a complete answer. You may also need to examine the four Mothers. In addition, the specific question may modify the answer. A loss would be bad news if the question involved money and investment, but it may well be good news if the question was concerned with losing an unpleasant neighbor or recovering from an illness. Consequently, use these meanings as a guide to help you while you're learning and to check your own findings. Once you've become familiar with the meanings of the figures in different placements, you'll seldom need to refer to these interpretations.

Meanings of the Judges and Witnesses

There are three positive Judges (Acquisitio, Fortuna Major, and Fortuna Minor), two negative Judges (Amissio and Carcer), and three neutral Judges (Populus, Via, and Conjunctio).

A positive Judge with positive Witnesses signifies a successful outcome. An example of this is Puer and Laetitia creating Acquisitio.

If a positive Judge is created from a positive Witness and a negative Witness, the outcome will be good, but there will be delays and problems before it occurs. Caput Draconis and Rubeus creating Fortuna Major is an example.

If the two Witnesses are positive, but the Judge is negative, the desired result will occur, but it will ultimately turn out to be an unhappy outcome. Puer and Caput Draconis creating Amissio is an example.

If the two Witnesses are negative, but the Judge is positive, the outcome will be good, but there will be a long struggle before it occurs. Amissio and Carcer creating Fortuna Major is an example.

If the Right Witness is positive and the Left Witness neutral or negative, success is unlikely.

If the Right Witness is neutral or negative and the Left Witness positive, the situation will deteriorate, but will then take a turn for the better.

Acquisitio (positive)—gain

On its own, Acquisitio indicates a favorable answer to the question. This is not surprising, as Acquisitio is ruled by the planet Jupiter.

Acquisitio is the Judge in any of the following combinations of Witnesses:

Left Witness   *Right Witness*

Populus (neutral)   *Acquisitio* (positive)
This combination is favorable for travel and legal matters, but unfavorable for anything else.

Acquisitio (positive)   *Populus* (neutral)
This combination is favorable for all matters, except for health.

Via (neutral)   *Amissio* (negative)
This combination is favorable for travel and legal matters, but modestly positive for anything else.

Amissio (negative)   *Via* (neutral)
This combination is mildly negative for all concerns.

Puer (positive)   *Laetitia* (positive)
This combination is modestly successful in all matters except speculation.

Laetitia (positive)   *Puer* (positive)
This combination is positive for all activities, except for dealings with opponents.

Rubeus (negative)   *Tristitia* (negative)
Despite the positive Judge, this combination is negative in all things, except dealings with competitors, opponents, and enemies.

Left Witness	*Right Witness*

Tristitia (negative)   *Rubeus* (negative)
This combination is negative for everything except legacies and inheritances.

Albus (neutral)   *Caput Draconis* (positive)
This combination is positive for all questions, except for those dealing with sickness.

Caput Draconis (positive)   *Albus* (neutral)
This combination is positive for all questions.

Puella (positive)   *Cauda Draconis* (negative)
This combination is mildly negative for all questions.

Cauda Draconis (negative)   *Puella* (positive)
This question is positive for everything, except matters relating to health.

Conjunctio (neutral)   *Fortuna Major* (positive)
This combination is positive for all questions.

Fortuna Major (positive)   *Conjunctio* (neutral)
This combination is positive for all matters, except those relating to illness.

Carcer (negative)   *Fortuna Minor* (positive)
This combination is mildly positive for all questions.

Fortuna Minor (positive)   *Carcer* (negative)
This combination is mildly positive for all questions, except those relating to sickness and dealings with adversaries.

Amissio (negative)—material loss

Amissio can indicate a positive outcome if the desired result is a loss. "Will I lose weight?" is a good example. The Witnesses need to be examined to determine the final outcome.

Amissio is the Judge in all of the following combinations of Witnesses:

Left Witness	*Right Witness*

Populus (neutral) *Amissio* (negative)
This combination is negative for all questions, except those relating to health and competitors, opponents and enemies.

Amissio (negative) *Populus* (neutral)
This combination is mildly negative for all questions.

Via (neutral) *Acquisitio* (positive)
This combination is mildly positive for all questions.

Acquisitio (positive) *Via* (neutral)
This combination is mildly positive for all questions.

Albus (neutral) *Laetitia* (positive)
This combination is mildly positive for all questions.

Laetitia (positive) *Albus* (neutral)
This combination is mildly positive for all questions, except those relating to sickness.

Puella (positive) *Tristitia* (negative)
This combination is mildly positive for all questions, except those dealing with competitors and adversaries.

Left Witness	*Right Witness*

Tristitia (negative)   *Puella* (positive)
This combination is mildly positive for questions relating to love, and negative for questions relating to enemies.

Puer (positive)   *Caput Draconis* (positive)
This combination is mildly positive for all questions, except those relating to love and romance.

Caput Draconis (positive)   *Puer* (positive)
This combination is mildly positive for all questions, except those relating to travel and dealings with competitors.

Rubeus (negative)   *Cauda Draconis* (negative)
This combination is negative for all questions, except for those involving marriage.

Cauda Draconis (negative)   *Rubeus* (negative)
This combination is negative for all questions, and especially so for questions relating to sickness.

Carcer (negative)   *Fortuna Major* (positive)
This combination is mildly positive for all questions, except those relating to love and marriage.

Fortuna Major (positive)   *Carcer* (negative)
This combination is neutral for most questions, but negative for questions relating to marriage and dealings with competitors and enemies.

Conjunctio (neutral)   *Fortuna Minor* (positive)
This combination is mildly positive for all questions.

Fortuna Minor (positive)   *Conjunctio* (neutral)
This combination is mildly positive for all questions.

Fortuna Major (positive)—good fortune

Fortuna Major usually indicates a successful outcome, especially if the two Witnesses are also positive. It may indicate a negative outcome if the answer to the question is not in the seeker's best interests.

Fortuna Major is the Judge in all of the following combinations of Witnesses:

Left Witness	*Right Witness*

Populus (neutral)   *Fortuna Major* (positive)
This is a favorable combination for almost all questions. However, it is not considered good for anything involving legal matters or inheritances. Populus indicates many opponents in the legal case and too many people seeking the inheritance.

Fortuna Major (positive)   *Populus* (neutral)
This is considered a favorable combination for all questions.

Via (neutral)   *Fortuna Minor* (positive)
This combination is favorable for questions involving travel and news, but unfavorable for anything else.

Fortuna Minor (positive)   *Via* (neutral)
This indicates a favorable outcome, except for questions involving progress in one's career. Career advancement is possible, but it will take a great deal of time and effort.

Conjunctio (neutral)   *Acquisitio* (positive)
This combination is favorable, except for questions involving inheritances and legal matters.

Left Witness	*Right Witness*

Acquisitio (positive)   *Conjunctio* (neutral)
This combination indicates a successful outcome for all questions.

Puella (positive)   *Laetitia* (positive)
This indicates an extremely favorable and happy outcome. It may well exceed the hopes of the person asking the question.

Laetitia (positive)   *Puella* (positive)
This combination indicates a successful outcome for all questions.

Caput Draconis (positive)   *Rubeus* (negative)
This indicates a moderately successful outcome for all questions, except those relating to money and personal matters. It usually indicates a slow, even negative start, but with a reasonable outcome.

Rubeus (negative)   *Caput Draconis* (positive)
This combination indicates a negative result for all questions. It indicates a good start, but with long-term negative results.

Cauda Draconis (negative)   *Puer* (positive)
This combination indicates a negative result. The start may be good, but ultimately you'll lose more than you gain.

Puer (positive)   *Cauda Draconis* (negative)
This combination is considered negative, except for questions dealing with rivals, opponents, and enemies.

Left Witness	*Right Witness*

Amissio (negative)   *Carcer* (negative)
This indicates a slightly negative outcome for all questions, except those involving communication or the conclusion of a venture.

Carcer (negative)   *Amissio* (negative)
This combination indicates a modestly favorable outcome for all questions, except those involving communication, inheritances, and legal matters.

Albus (neutral)   *Tristitia* (negative)
This combination indicates a slightly negative outcome to all questions, except those involving money and investments.

Tristitia (negative)   *Albus* (neutral)
This combination indicates a modestly favorable outcome for all questions.

Fortuna Minor (positive)—good luck

Fortuna Minor indicates partial success. The Witnesses need to be examined to determine how successful the outcome will be.

Fortuna Minor is the Judge in all of the following combinations:

Left Witness	*Right Witness*

Populus (neutral)   *Fortuna Minor* (positive)
This combination indicates a moderately successful outcome for all questions, except those that relate to inheritances and legal matters.

Left Witness	*Right Witness*

Fortuna Minor (positive) *Populus* (neutral)
This combination is favorable for all questions, except those
that relate to work done for us by others.

Carcer (negative) *Acquisitio* (positive)
This combination is favorable for all questions, except
those relating to marriage, career, and the final outcome of
a project that is already underway.

Acquisitio (positive) *Carcer* (negative)
This combination is favorable for all questions, except those
relating to communication.

Rubeus (negative) *Laetitia* (positive)
This combination is considered negative for all questions,
except those involving conflict with others. You will win the
fight, but the price will be high.

Laetitia (positive) *Rubeus* (negative)
This combination is considered favorable for all questions.
The matter might prove difficult at first, but success will
occur.

Puer (positive) *Tristitia* (negative)
This combination is considered negative, except for questions relating to marriage and long-term relationships.

Tristitia (negative) *Puer* (positive)
This combination is mildly positive for all questions, except
those relating to competitors, rivals, enemies, and legal
concerns.

Left Witness	Right Witness

Puella (positive)   *Caput Draconis* (positive)
This combination is considered favorable for all questions. The outcome will be especially good for any questions relating to love.

Caput Draconis (positive)   *Puella* (positive)
This combination is considered favorable for all questions, except those relating to love and romance.

Albus (neutral)   *Cauda Draconis* (negative)
This combination is considered favorable for all questions. Success will come quickly after a slow start.

Cauda Draconis (negative)   *Albus* (neutral)
This combination is considered negative for all questions.

Conjunctio (neutral)   *Amissio* (negative)
This combination indicates a modestly favorable outcome for all questions.

Amissio (negative)   *Conjunctio* (neutral)
This combination is considered negative for all questions. However, if the question involves a wedding, this combination is a sign that it will take place.

Via (neutral)   *Fortuna Major* (positive)
This combination is favorable for questions relating to travel and personal concerns. However, it is negative for everything else.

Fortuna Major (positive)   *Via* (neutral)
This combination indicates a favorable outcome for all questions.

Populus (neutral)—dealings with others

Populus is the Judge who appears more than any other. The Witnesses need to be examined carefully, as they determine the outcome in every case.

Populus is the Judge in all of the following combinations:

Left Witness   *Right Witness*

Acquisitio (positive)   *Acquisitio* (positive)
This combination indicates a favorable outcome for all questions, except those that relate to career.

Populus (neutral)   *Populus* (neutral)
This combination is negative for questions relating to inheritances, legal matters, and the final result of a project that is already underway. It is considered favorable for all other questions.

Laetitia (positive)   *Laetitia* (positive)
This combination indicates success, along with a great deal of happiness and good fortune.

Amissio (negative)   *Amissio* (negative)
This combination is considered negative for all questions.

Caput Draconis (positive)   *Caput Draconis* (positive)
This combination indicates a successful outcome for any question. Caput Draconis confers spiritual benefits to the outcome, if that is required.

Tristitia (negative)   *Tristitia* (negative)
This combination is considered negative for all questions. It causes frustration, disruption, and delays.

Left Witness	Right Witness

Puella (positive)   *Puella* (positive)
This combination indicates a successful outcome, aided by the charm and people skills provided by Venus.

Cauda Draconis (negative)   *Cauda Draconis* (negative)
This combination is considered negative for all questions. This may be due to karmic debts created in previous lifetimes.

Albus (neutral)   *Albus* (neutral)
This combination indicates a favorable outcome for all questions. The wisdom and communication skills of Mercury help create a highly beneficial outcome.

Puer (positive)   *Puer* (positive)
This combination is considered negative, except for questions involving travel, career, and competitive activities, such as sports.

Fortuna Major (positive)   *Fortuna Major* (positive)
This combination indicates a successful outcome for all questions, except those involving travel. This is because Populus indicates possible accidents when too many people travel at the same time.

Fortuna Minor (positive)   *Fortuna Minor* (positive)
This combination indicates a moderately favorable outcome for all questions, except those relating to the outcome of a project that is already underway.

Rubeus (negative)   *Rubeus* (negative)
This combination indicates a negative outcome for all questions.

Left Witness   *Right Witness*

Via (neutral)   *Via* (neutral)
This combination indicates a successful outcome for all questions, except those relating to career.

Conjunctio (neutral)   *Conjunctio* (neutral)
This combination indicates a successful outcome to all questions. This is caused by the eloquence and communication skills provided by Mercury.

Carcer (negative)   *Carcer* (negative)
This combination is considered negative for questions relating to career, love, and legal matters. However, it is considered positive for all other questions. Saturn provides persistence and a cautious, practical approach.

Via (neutral)—forward movement

The Witnesses need to be examined carefully when Via is the Judge. They largely determine the answer to the question.

Left Witness   *Right Witness*

Via (neutral)   *Populus* (neutral)
This combination indicates a mildly negative outcome to all questions, because of the number of people involved.

Populus (neutral)   *Via* (neutral)
This combination indicates a mildly positive outcome to all questions, except those relating to inheritances and career.

Acquisitio (positive)   *Amissio* (negative)
This combination is favorable for all questions.

Left Witness   *Right Witness*

Amissio (negative)   *Acquisitio* (positive)
This combination is considered negative for all questions, except those involving communication and customer service.

Laetitia (positive)   *Caput Draconis* (positive)
This combination is favorable for all questions.

Caput Draconis (positive)   *Laetitia* (positive)
This combination is favorable for all questions, except those dealing with career.

Tristitia (negative)   *Cauda Draconis* (negative)
This combination is negative for all questions, except legal matters, which will go in your favor.

Cauda Draconis (negative)   *Tristitia* (negative)
This combination is considered negative for all questions.

Puella (positive)   *Rubeus* (negative)
This combination is considered favorable for all questions. This is because, in this instance, Venus and Mars work well together.

Rubeus (negative)   *Puella* (positive)
This combination is considered negative for all questions, except those relating to love and romance. However, even in this case, the love affair will have its share of ups and downs.

Puer (positive)   *Albus* (neutral)
This combination is considered negative for all questions. This is because the Mercury/Mars combination creates impatience and impulsiveness.

Left Witness	*Right Witness*

Albus (neutral)   *Puer* (positive)
This combination is favorable for all questions, except those involving new ventures that have not yet started.

Conjunctio (neutral)   *Carcer* (negative)
This combination is favorable for all questions, as long as thought and patience are utilized.

Carcer (negative)   *Conjunctio* (neutral)
This combination is negative for all questions, except those dealing with legal matters and marriage.

Fortuna Major (positive)   *Fortuna Minor* (positive)
This combination is favorable for all questions, except those involving everyday life.

Fortuna Minor (positive)   *Fortuna Major* (positive)
This combination is favorable for all questions, except those relating to career and legal concerns.

Conjunctio (neutral)—union

Conjunctio relates to cooperation, discussion, committees, and agreement. It indicates that the outcome needs more than one person to proceed.

Conjunctio is the Judge in all of the following combinations:

Left Witness	*Right Witness*

Conjunctio (neutral)   *Populus* (neutral)
This combination is moderately adverse for all questions, except those relating to inheritances and legal matters.

Left Witness	Right Witness

Populus (neutral)   *Conjunctio* (neutral)
This combination is mildly negative for all questions, except those relating to opponents, competitors, and enemies.

Acquisitio (positive)   *Fortuna Major* (positive)
This combination is favorable for all questions, except those relating to opponents, competitors, and enemies. The Jupiter/Sun combination can create overconfidence when dealing with potential rivals.

Fortuna Major (positive)   *Acquisitio* (positive)
This combination is extremely positive for all questions.

Amissio (negative)   *Fortuna Minor* (positive)
This combination is considered negative for all questions. Fortuna Minor may bring a small piece of luck, but the outcome will still be negative.

Fortuna Minor (positive)   *Amissio* (negative)
This combination is considered negative for all questions, except those involving, career, love, and interaction with rivals and competitors.

Laetitia (positive)   *Cauda Draconis* (negative)
This combination is favorable for all questions. There will be obstacles initially, but the outcome will be good.

Cauda Draconis (negative)   *Laetitia* (positive)
This combination is considered negative for all questions, except those dealing with communication and travel.

Left Witness	*Right Witness*

Caput Draconis (positive)   *Tristitia* (negative)
This combination is considered unfavorable for all questions.

Tristitia (negative)   *Caput Draconis* (positive)
This combination is favorable for all questions. Tristitia indicates delays at the start, but Caput Draconis promises a successful outcome.

Rubeus (negative)   *Albus* (neutral)
This combination is favorable for all questions.

Albus (neutral)   *Rubeus* (negative)
This combination is unfavorable for all questions.

Via (neutral)   *Carcer* (negative)
This combination is slightly negative for all questions, except those relating to inheritances, marriage, and legal matters.

Carcer (negative)   *Via* (neutral)
This combination is slightly negative for all questions, except for those relating to communications, marriage, and dealings with adversaries.

Carcer (negative)—restriction

Carcer relates to bondage, restrictions, limitations, obligations, duty, and legal contracts.

Left Witness	*Right Witness*

Carcer (negative)   *Populus* (neutral)
This combination is good for finances and love, but negative for everything else.

Left Witness   **Right Witness**

Populus (neutral)   *Carcer* (negative)
This combination is negative for dealings with competitors, opponents, and adversaries, and neutral for all other questions.

Acquisitio (positive)   *Fortuna Minor* (positive)
This combination is mildly positive for all questions, except those dealing with legal matters and enemies.

Fortuna Minor (positive)   *Acquisitio* (positive)
This combination is mildly positive for all questions, except those dealing with illnesses.

Amissio (negative)   *Fortuna Major* (positive)
This combination is mildly positive for all questions.

Fortuna Major (positive)   *Amissio* (negative)
This combination is mildly negative for all questions.

Laetitia (positive)   *Tristitia* (negative)
This combination is positive for questions relating to inheritances and legacies, but is negative for everything else.

Tristitia (negative)   *Laetitia* (positive)
This combination is negative for questions relating to love and marriage, but mildly positive for everything else.

Puella (positive)   *Albus* (neutral)
This combination is negative for questions relating to marriage, but is mildly positive for everything else.

Left Witness	*Right Witness*

Albus (neutral) *Puella* (positive)
This combination is mildly positive for all questions.

Rubeus (negative) *Puer* (positive)
This combination is negative for all questions.

Puer (positive) *Rubeus* (negative)
This combination is negative for questions relating to travel and romance, and neutral for all other questions.

Caput Draconis (positive) *Cauda Draconis* (negative)
This combination is negative for all questions.

Cauda Draconis (negative) *Caput Draconis* (positive)
This combination is negative for all questions relating to love and romance, and mildly positive for everything else.

Conjunctio (neutral) *Via* (neutral)
This combination is negative for all questions, except those dealing with competitors and adversaries.

Via (neutral) *Conjunctio* (neutral)
This combination is mildly positive for all questions, except those relating to work and career.

five

Astrological Geomancy

Creating and interpreting the shield chart is a useful way to gain insight into a particular situation, and to discover how to benefit from it. However, there are occasions when much more detail is required. Because of this, a system was devised that combines geomancy and astrology. This broadens the scope of the reading enormously, as astrology covers every area of life.

Astrology began about five thousand years ago in Mesopotamia. Because life was short, brutal, and frequently dangerous, people became interested in a variety of methods that might provide glimpses of the future. As their gods and goddesses lived in the heavens, it's not surprising that people spent a great deal of time watching the changing patterns in the night sky. They were particularly fascinated with the planets, and studied their movements across the sky. They believed that the planets were their gods.

About four thousand years ago, astrologers divided the heavens into twelve equal parts, and these became the signs of the zodiac. On the first day of spring, the Sun was in Aries, and as the year progressed, it moved into each of the other signs in turn, spending approximately one month in each sign. The signs are simply divisions in space, each taking up thirty degrees of a huge, imaginary circle known as the ecliptic. The ecliptic is the path that the planets appear to follow through the heavens.

There are also twelve houses in astrology. This is an imaginary circle in the sky above your head. Unlike the signs of the zodiac, the houses do not move, but remain fixed in time and space. This is a concept that dates from the time of Ptolemy (fl. 127–145 CE). Ptolemy was a Greek astronomer, and author of a book called *Almagest* (The Greatest), which was the most influential book on astronomy until the sixteenth century. Ptolemy related the houses to twelve basic areas of life. The system that the astrologers of Ptolemy's day devised is still used by astrologers today.

The houses are the most important area of geomantic astrology. As there are twelve houses, the first twelve figures created in answering a question (Mothers, Daughters, and Nieces) are placed into each house. The first Mother created goes into the first house, and the other figures go into their respective houses in order of creation. Once the chart has been created, it can be interpreted. Before we can do that, however, we need to know what each house represents.

Ratings of the Figures in the Twelve Houses

The sixteen figures are always strongest in the houses that they rule. They become progressively less powerful when located in other houses. See the chart on the next page.

Nowadays, the astrological geomantic chart consists of a circle divided into twelve equal segments. Originally, it was square in shape. Traditionally, the eastern horizon is always drawn on the left-hand side of the circle at the place where the hour hand of a clock indicates nine o'clock. The segment between eight o'clock and nine o'clock represents the first house. The segment between seven and eight o'clock is the second house. The other houses continue in a counterclockwise order. The twelfth house completes the circle and comprises the segment between nine and ten o'clock.

How to Prepare an Astrological Geomantic Chart

The basic instructions for creating an astrological geomantic chart are the same as for creating the shield chart. However, only the four Mothers, four Daughters, and four Nieces go into the chart. In practice, you should also create the Witnesses and the Judge to provide additional information.

First, a question needs to be formulated, and thought about, while the four Mothers are being created. Let's assume you're asking a question about travel. You might ask, "Should I travel to Venice this summer?"

Figure	Strongest	Strong	Favorable	Weak	Weakest
Puer	1, 8	10	5	4	2, 7
Amissio	2, 7	12	9, 11	6	1, 8
Albus	3	6	4, 10	12	9
Populus	4	2	12	8	10
Fortuna Major	5	1	8	7	11
Conjunctio	6	3	4, 10	12	9
Puella	7, 2	12	9, 11	6	1, 8
Rubeus	8, 1	10	5	4	2, 7
Acquisitio	9, 12	4	1, 2, 7	10	3, 6
Carcer	10, 11	7	3, 6	1	4, 5
Tristitia	11, 10	7	3, 6	1	4, 5
Laetitia	12, 9	4	1, 2, 7	10	3, 6
Cauda Draconis		9		3	
Caput Draconis		3		9	
Fortuna Minor	5	1	8	7	11
Via	4	2	12	8	10

You cast the following four Mothers:

First Mother	Second Mother	Third Mother	Fourth Mother
O O	O	O O	O
O O	O O	O O	O O
O	O O	O O	O
O O	O	O	O O
Albus	Carcer	Tristitia	Amissio

From this you create the four Daughters:

O O	O O	O	O O
O	O O	O O	O
O O	O O	O O	O
O	O O	O	O O
Acquisitio	Populus	Carcer	Conjunctio

Finally, the four Nieces are created:

O	O	O O	O
O O	O O	O	O
O	O	O O	O
O	O	O	O
Puella	Puella	Acquisitio	Via

These twelve figures are placed in their respective houses (see the chart on the next page).

Your question related to extensive travel, which is a ninth-house matter. Puella is in this position. This is a positive sign for short trips, rather than extensive travel.

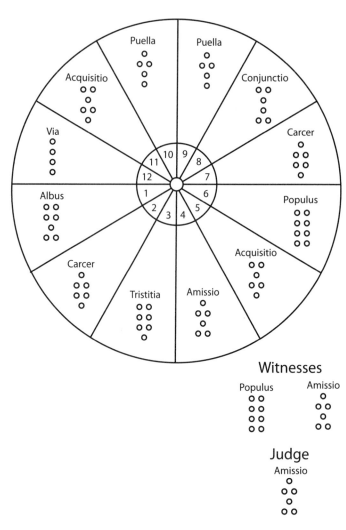

Chart 5A

However, looking at a single figure is exactly the same as relying solely on the Judge in the shield chart. You also need to look at the figure in the first house, as this indicates you, and the figure in the fourth house, which indicates how the trip will finish.

Albus in the first house is a positive figure, too, indicating a quiet, peaceful, and pleasant vacation. However, Amissio is in the fourth house. This indicates a loss of some sort. You might lose something or have some money stolen, for instance. On the other hand, you might lose your heart to an attractive Italian. One of these scenarios is bad, but the other may be good, depending on whether or not you're looking for a new relationship. The loss could be in any area of your life. It might indicate a loss of innocence, a loss of a long-held belief, or possibly the loss of a friendship.

Amissio puts a totally different slant on the question. If you were planning to take the trip with a good friend, the friendship might end. Regardless, if you took the trip this summer, you would experience a loss of some sort. Most of the trip would be happy and live up to your expectations, but the loss could prove costly. You might think it a good idea to delay the visit to Venice, and plan a different vacation this year.

So far, this is similar to creating a shield chart, as you are still using three figures to answer your question. You can, if you wish, double this by including the two Witnesses and the Judge.

In the example above, we'd use the four Nieces to create these extra figures. These are:

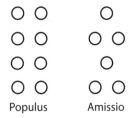

Populus   Amissio

These then create the Judge:

Amissio

The two Witnesses and the Judge are usually placed in the center of the horoscope chart. These figures provide more information relating to the proposed trip to Venice.

Amissio, the Judge, indicates a loss. This could be anything from losing your heart, to a loss of health or money. As Amissio is also the Right Witness, this unfortunate figure appears three times in relation to your question. Populus, the Left Witness, can be either positive or negative, depending on the other figures. As both the Right Witness and the Judge are negative, Populus is negative in this reading, too. The loss is virtually guaranteed if the trip goes ahead this summer, and the best decision is to postpone the trip to avoid any difficulty or loss.

Here is another example. Let's suppose you've been unwell for some time, and are wondering when your health will improve. You might ask, "Will my health improve markedly in the next three months?"

You cast the four Mothers, and then create the other figures from them:

First Mother	Second Mother	Third Mother	Fourth Mother
O O	O	O O	O O
O	O	O O	O
O	O O	O	O O
O O	O	O	O
Conjunctio	Puer	Fortuna Major	Acquisitio

Once the figures have been created, they can be placed into the astrological chart (see the next two pages).

The two Witnesses (Puer—left, and Rubeus—right) and the Judge (Carcer) are placed in the center of the circle.

You start by looking at the first house, which represents you. You have Conjunctio in this position. Conjunctio is relatively passive, and can be favorable or unfavorable, depending on the situation. As it is favorable in matters concerning something that has been lost, it can be considered favorable in this situation, as your health has effectively been lost. Conjunctio can also be found in the tenth house, which relates to your reputation, self-esteem, and standing in the community. As Conjunctio is favorable in the tenth house, it appears that regaining your health is important to you, as it helps you maintain your confidence and self-esteem. What other people may think is also important to you.

First Daughter   Second Daughter   Third Daughter   Fourth Daughter

Rubeus   Fortuna Minor   Amissio   Caput Draconis

First Niece   Second Niece   Third Niece   Fourth Niece

Puella   Conjunctio   Carcer   Puer

Left Witness   Right Witness

Puer   Rubeus

The Judge

Carcer

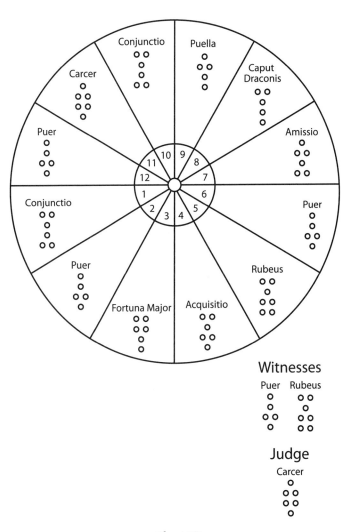

Chart 5B

Health is a sixth-house concern. Puer is in this position. This figure usually indicates impulsiveness and sudden change. However, most of Puer's problems occur when the person acts without thinking. If you remain positive and focus on regaining your health, this figure is a favorable one.

You have Acquisitio in the fourth house. This is usually a figure of success, and it shows that something you are seeking is about to occur. Unfortunately, it is an unfavorable figure as far as health is concerned, as in this situation you want to lose something (ill health).

These three figures tend to indicate a temporary improvement, but not a permanent cure, at least not in the next three months. Because the answer isn't clear, it can be helpful to look at the Judge and the two Witnesses.

The Judge is Carcer. Carcer always indicates a delay. It is usually a negative figure, but can be helpful in matters concerning stability.

The Left Witness is Puer. This represents both the future and the question. Unfortunately, Puer is unfavorable as far as this question is concerned. Admittedly, it can be favorable when change is desired, but it also relates to conflict, sudden change, and upheaval.

The Right Witness is Rubeus, which is an unfortunate figure to have in this position. It is a difficult figure at the best of times, but it can be favorable if the question relates to sexuality, passion, and pleasure. Unfortunately, none of these relate to this particular question.

Nothing in this reading indicates that your health will be restored in the next three months. Consequently, you should pay attention to your doctor, and accept that it will take longer than you wish for your health to improve.

In this chapter we have looked at the twelve houses of astrology. To complete the chart, we need to add the seven planets and the twelve zodiac signs. We will do this in the next chapter.

The Twelve Houses

The twelve houses represent different aspects of a person's everyday life. In astrology, the first house occupies the area of a circle between eight and nine o'clock, if the circle were considered to be a clock. The second house is between seven and eight o'clock, and the other houses continue in a counterclockwise direction to complete 360 degrees.

The Sun takes twenty-four hours to pass through the twelve houses, spending approximately two hours in each house.

First House

The first house, known as the Ascendant, reveals the person's personality, temperament, vitality, health, and individuality. It reveals how the person will express himself or herself. It also shows his or her approach to life.

Second House

The second house indicates possessions, financial matters, and the person's ability to earn money. It also reveals the person's self-esteem, personal values, and his or her inner resources.

Third House

The third house relates to all types of communication and self-expression. It relates to learning, mental activity, and the written and spoken word. As it also relates to transportation, short journeys are also considered part of the third house. This house also relates to the person's brothers and sisters, close relatives, neighbors, and the environment the person lives in. It is strongly associated with everyday affairs.

Fourth House

The fourth house relates to home, family, and ancestry. It also relates to physical property and the parent who had the more important influence on the person. The fourth house also indicates the ending of something. Because of this, it also relates to old age. In geomancy, the fourth house indicates the conclusion, or result, of the question.

Fifth House

The fifth house relates to love and romance, children, pleasure, entertainment, speculation, physical activity, and creativity. It reveals the person's originality and initiative, and the amount of love he or she is prepared to offer. This includes courtship, marriage, and lovemaking.

Sixth House

The sixth house relates to employment, work colleagues, obligations, service to others, and personal health. The tenth house relates to the person's career, but the sixth house looks after the everyday aspects of his or her work.

Seventh House

The seventh house relates to all types of partnerships, agreements, contracts, and dealings with the public. It reveals your attitude towards close relationships and your ability to get along and cooperate with others. Consequently, it relates to a person's partner. As the seventh house is concerned with all types of relationships, this house can also relate to opponents, competitors, and known enemies.

Eighth House

The eighth house indicates the level of support the person will receive from others. This support can be financial, physical, or spiritual, and includes the earning ability of the person's partner, as well as inheritances. It also relates to business transactions that involve other people's money. The eighth house also relates to taxes, insurance, sex, surgery, death, and anything that is hidden, including the occult.

Ninth House

The ninth house relates to philosophy, religion, science, art, higher learning, moral and legal concerns, and the communication of ideas. It relates to all large-scale activities. The ninth house also relates to extensive travel. (The third house relates to short trips.)

Tenth House

The tenth house reveals the person's reputation, honor, authority, status, profession, and standing in the community. It also shows the person's achievements, and the degree of influence he or she has. All of this also relates to the person's self-esteem. The tenth house also relates to the person's mother or father.

Eleventh House

The eleventh house relates to friends, acquaintances, and all non-romantic relationships. It relates to clubs, social organizations, and any philanthropic or humanitarian groups the person may belong to. It also relates to the person's hopes, aspirations, desires, and dreams, as well as situations over which he or she has no control.

Twelfth House

The twelfth house relates to the person's latent talents and his or her subconscious mind. It also reveals any secrets the person might prefer to keep hidden. (This house also relates to secret enemies. Open enemies are related to the seventh house.) The twelfth house also relates to limitations, fears, restrictions, confinement, and sorrows.

The Sixteen Figures in the Twelve Houses

The best way to learn the meanings of the figures in the different houses is to study the individual figures and relate them to the activities of the various houses. In the past, most books included lengthy, incredibly fatalistic lists explaining what each figure meant in different houses.

Remember that it's rare for one house to be looked at in isolation, as usually a number of houses are involved in any divination. Here are the traditional meanings for the figures in the houses. These interpretations are fatalistic, and reflect the times in which they were written. Consequently, a prediction of death (Amissio in the first house), for instance, is more likely to indicate an illness today than an actual death.

I have deliberately left out interpretations that relate to dealings with kings and other nobles (tenth house). These may have been important in Renaissance times, but they are largely irrelevant today. For the same reason, I have not included any information about honest or dishonest servants (sixth house), the activities of thieves (second house), and whether or not someone who is imprisoned will die, remain in prison, escape, or obtain his freedom by other means (twelfth house).

Via in the Twelve Houses

1. A long and happy life.
2. Increase in fortune. Something that has been lost or stolen will be recovered.
3. Enjoyable travel. Many happy times with brothers and other relatives.
4. A good and honest father. Fortunes improve.
5. Male children. A son will be born.
6. Protection against illness and disease.
7. A long and happy marriage with a beautiful partner.
8. Someone thought to be dead is still alive. Large legacy.
9. Extensive travel. Considerable profit. Interest in philosophy and religion.
10. A highly respected mother. Honor, recognition, and increased status.

11. Many useful friends. Financial rewards gained from other countries.

12. Many ineffective enemies. Protection from harm.

Caput Draconis in the Twelve Houses

1. A long, happy, prosperous, and powerful life.

2. Possibility of wealth and prosperity.

3. Travel, dealings with brothers, interest in religion, and a good marriage.

4. Inheritances. Father lives to a ripe old age.

5. Children, honor, and possible fame. If a child is expected, it will be a boy.

6. Illness, but a good doctor restores your health.

7. Possibility of more than one marriage. Financial benefits come from women.

8. Inheritances and money from other sources. Someone close to you dies and leaves you money.

9. Extensive travel. Growth in knowledge, wisdom, and spirituality.

10. Dealings with important people. A good mother. A happy, contented life.

11. Popularity. Many pleasant social occasions with friends. Opportunity for wealth.

12. A strong feminine influence. Secret enemies who cannot harm you.

Puella in the Twelve Houses

1. Comparatively short life. Be careful in dealings with the opposite sex.

2. Your fortunes do not increase or decrease at this time.

3. Pleasant social activities. Enjoyable travel. Happy times with siblings.

4. Small inheritance. A good harvest.

5. Favors from women. If someone is pregnant, the child will be a girl.

6. Someone who is extremely unwell will make a quick, almost miraculous, recovery.

7. A beautiful wife remains faithful despite the attentions of several admirers.

8. Someone who is thought to be dead is actually still alive. A small dowry.

9. Short travel. A good time for singing and dancing.

10. Help from influential women.

11. Many male and female friends.

12. Enemies are few, but there will be problems with women.

Fortuna Major in the Twelve Houses

1. A long, happy, contented life.

2. Profit and wealth.

3. Enjoyable travel, good friends, and pleasant times with relatives.

4. A highly respected father. A good inheritance.

5. Happy family life. Children. Possibility of fame.

6. Good health, with quick recovery from any illnesses.

7. A good marriage. Success over opponents.

8. Painless and natural death or ending to a situation. Partner receives a good legacy.

9. Extensive, successful, and enjoyable travel. Development of spirituality, intuition, and knowledge.

10. Honor and recognition. A long-lived, good mother.

11. Happiness, surrounded by good, true friends and a loving family.

12. Success over enemies.

Puer in the Twelve Houses

1. An eventful life with many problems. A good soldier.

2. Money must be earned, as there is no inheritance.

3. Dangerous travel. Opportunity to increase your reputation in the community.

4. Wealth acquired in a rather dubious manner.

5. Good children, who will do well financially. If someone is pregnant, the baby will be a boy.

6. Possibility of accidents and illness. Fortunately, recovery is quick and easy.

7. A strong, honest, and courageous wife.

8. A missing person is alive. A quick death.

9. Dangerous but highly successful travel. Opportunity to learn natural sciences, medicine, or the arts.

10. Changes in fortune. Danger to the mother.

11. Friendship with influential people. Profit acquired in a doubtful manner.

12. Dangerous enemies.

Acquisitio in the Twelve Houses

1. A long life, and a happy and contented old age.

2. Wealth and security. Anything that has been lost or stolen will be returned.

3. A happy and successful family life. Enjoyable travel. Honest and sincere friends.

4. Inheritances, especially from parents. Substantial assets.

5. Birth of a child who is more likely to be male than female.

6. Serious illness, but experienced doctors ensure a successful recovery.

7. A wealthy woman. Possibility of legal problems and/or a love affair.

8. Death of person being inquired about. Substantial inheritance.

9. Lengthy, but highly profitable, travel. Knowledge gained from experienced teachers.

10. Wealthy and happy mother. Legal matters work out favorably. Good business opportunities.

11. Many friendships that result in profitable opportunities. Someone may favor you with his or her business.

12. Powerful enemies. Lost animals, especially household pets, found.

Carcer in the Twelve Houses

1. A short life. Dealings with someone who is universally disliked.

2. Financial problems.

3. Problems with relatives. Any travel proves disappointing.

4. Possible legacy fails to eventuate. Father is a bad influence.

5. Difficulties with children. Gossip and slander.

6. Health problems.

7. Problems between husband and wife.

8. Sudden death. Money has to be earned.

9. A traveler will fail to return home. A bad conscience causes feelings of guilt and self-loathing.

10. Problems with authority.

11. Lack of true friends.

12. Enemies cause misfortune.

Tristitia in the Twelve Houses

1. An average-length life, but one full of problems.

2. Money comes, but is hidden away and not used.

3. Difficult and dangerous travel.

4. Expected legacy fails to arrive. A long-lived, money-focused father.

5. If someone is pregnant, the baby will be a girl. Little chance of recognition or fame.

6. Someone who is ill will die.

7. Possibility that the wife will die.

8. Death after a long and painful illness. The wife inherits.

9. Lengthy, but unfortunate, travel. Potential to learn.

10. Mother will have a long life. Obstacles, delays, and frustrations.

11. Few friends, and one is likely to die.

12. No enemies. Constant difficulties.

Cauda Draconis in the Twelve Houses

1. Ill fortune, troubles, losses, and disappointments.

2. Financial struggle.

3. Disappointment in travel. Disagreements with siblings.

4. Expected money fails to materialize. Hard work and much sorrow.

5. Dealings with children, much of it difficult.

6. Health problems.

7. Marital difficulties. Enemies cause mischief that affects your reputation.

8. Small inheritance or dowry. Loss of goods.

9. Extensive travel that fails to pay off. Suspicion and loss of faith.

10. Overlooked for promotion, honor, and prestige.

11. Friends hard to find. Nothing achieved without backbreaking work.

12. Enemies cause difficulties.

Conjunctio in the Twelve Houses

1. A long and happy life. Many friends.

2. A comfortable life. Anything lost or stolen will be recovered.

3. Travel with mixed success.

4. Reasonable inheritance. A good, intelligent father.

5. Intelligent children. If the question involves pregnancy, the child will be a boy. Good reputation.

6. Lengthy illness that is attended to by experienced doctors.

7. An intelligent wife. Possibility of litigation.

8. Death of the person being inquired after. Possible financial advantage may accrue.

9. Lengthy travel. Interest in spiritual matters.

10. A good and wise mother.

11. Many friends, some highly influential.

12. Cunning enemies. Success in averting any danger.

Amissio in the Twelve Houses

1. A patient is unlikely to recover.

2. A difficult financial situation, with the possibility of a major loss. Poverty.

3. Someone may try to cheat you out of something. Possible death of a close relative.

4. Inheritance from father is likely to be small and does not last for long.

5. Possible miscarriage, or death of a child. Someone may slander you.

6. The person who is ill makes a full recovery.

7. Problems with a difficult wife. Possible legal action will be taken against you.

8. Death of an acquaintance or former friend.

9. Little or no travel, which is fortunate, as no benefit will come from it. Someone who finds it hard to make up his or her mind.

10. Possibility of damaging your reputation and standing in the community. Possible death of mother.

11. You are likely to lose friends at this time, and you find it hard to make new friends.

12. Your enemies will be defeated.

Albus in the Twelve Houses

1. An entertaining conversationalist. Someone who is temporarily unwell.

2. Money gained from some form of entertainment. Lost or stolen articles returned or discovered.

3. Short but difficult travel. Someone may be cheating.

4. Unlikelihood of any inheritance from parents.

5. Possible miscarriage. Likelihood that others are talking about you behind your back.

6. Lengthy health problems.

7. A loving wife who is unlikely to bear children. Possibility of legal action.

8. Death of person being inquired about. Small inheritance obtained with difficulty.

9. Lengthy travel that produces little in the way of profit. Everything takes longer and is more difficult than anticipated.

10. Difficulties in career or business. You will have to extricate yourself, as there will be little help from others.

11. False friends, deception, and ups and downs financially.

12. Enemies, known or unknown, will be unable to hurt you.

Fortuna Minor in the Twelve Houses

1. A lengthy life, but with minor illnesses along the way.

2. Without care and attention, expenses can easily exceed income.

3. Difficulties with relatives. Potential danger while traveling averted.

4. Loss of money inherited from father and other relatives. Problems in finding anything that has been lost or stolen.

5. If someone is pregnant, the child will be a girl. Recognition and honor, but with little tangible reward.

6. Illness overcome.

7. Procrastination. Marriage to a good, well-bred woman.

8. Someone close to you dies in another country. Problems in receiving money owed.

9. Problems connected to lengthy travel. Extra research required in learning the full story.

10. Financial ups and downs. Powerful people offer little help.

11. Pleasant times with people who have little or no influence. Slight financial improvement.

12. Expect change. Enemies can cause temporary difficulties.

Rubeus in the Twelve Houses

1. A short life with a violent end.

2. Poverty caused by thieves and cheats.

3. Difficult relatives, short travel, and the possibility that someone will betray you.

4. Loss of inheritance. Death of father.

5. Difficulties with children.

6. Death caused by a doctor's error.

7. A quarrelsome, difficult wife. Someone will conspire to take advantage of you.

8. The person inquired after is dead. Forcible death, such as execution or hanging.

9. Difficult travel. Possibility of robbery or imprisonment.

10. Dealings with cheats, swindlers, and usurers. Sudden death of mother.

11. Numerous obstacles to progress. Many enemies.

12. Many problems and difficulties. Powerful enemies conspire against you.

Laetitia in the Twelve Houses

1. A long, happy, successful life.

2. Possibility of great wealth, but expenses will be high.

3. Pleasant travel, and an enjoyable home and family life.

4. Possessions, inheritance, and good financial opportunities.

5. Well-behaved children. If someone is pregnant, the child will be a girl.

6. An ill person recovers.

7. Success in all matters concerning love.

8. Legacies.

9. Extensive travel. Opportunities to develop intuitively.

10. Dealings with like-minded people. If the mother is a widow, she will remarry.

11. Protection provided by well-placed friends.

12. Victory over one's enemies.

Populus in the Twelve Houses

1. An average lifespan. Changes in fortune.

2. Reasonable wealth, achieved with great effort.

3. Dealings with relatives. Beware of a loss caused by someone cheating you.

4. Money earned from overseas trade. Difficulty in receiving money that is owed.

5. A modest lifestyle. Possibility of a miscarriage.

6. Potential for illness. Choose your doctor carefully.

7. Possibility of infidelity.

8. A quick and sudden death. A small dowry.

9. Laziness causes problems. Little interest in spiritual matters.

10. Potential losses. An unwell mother.

11. Many people flatter you, but you have only a few true friends. Do not expect favors from others.

12. Your enemies are weak and ineffectual. Danger from water.

six

Planets and Signs

Thousands of years ago, when astrologers first studied the heavens, they observed stars that appeared to stay in one place, as well as moving bodies that followed a set path through the sky. They named the moving bodies *planets*, or wanderers.

Five thousand years ago, the ancient Babylonians compared the movements of the planets through a garden of fixed stars to "stray goats" that wandered freely, but were beholden to the shepherd god, Marduk. They developed a mythology around the planets based on their colors and movements. Shamash, the Sun, was a charioteer who carried light across the sky from morning until night. Sin, the Moon, was considered wise, as she was able to change shape. At one time, she was married to Shamash, but had left him, as she preferred to travel on her own. Because at certain times of the month her shape resembled a sickle, she became associated with agriculture. She also became associated with seafarers, as her reflection could be seen on the water.

Mercury is never more than twenty-five degrees away from the Sun and is often hard to see. It was called *gud-ud*, or *Mushtaddallu*, which means "the messenger." Venus also follows the Sun, and was called *dil-bad*, which means "proclaimer." Because Venus was the first star to be seen in the night sky, and often rose before dawn, Venus became associated with love and romance. The Babylonians considered dusk and dawn to be the best times at which to make love.

Mars appears to be red. Because of this, he is associated with the god Nergal, as well as heat, war, and death. Jupiter had two names: *molobabar* ("most high god") and *sag-me-gar* ("chief oracle-giver"). The Babylonians found it fascinating that Jupiter disappeared from sight for one month every year. Saturn became associated with time, as it took more than twenty-nine years to pass through every sign of the zodiac. Saturn was called *kakkab shamshi* ("Star of the Sun").

Ptolemy, the Alexandrian astrologer, associated the five known planets, plus the Sun and Moon, with the different signs of the zodiac. The qualities associated with each planet were passed on to the sign associated with it. Mars, for instance, was known as the "warrior planet." It is exalted in Aries, and gives Arians the attributes of courage, bravery, and restlessness.

The Signs

Most people are familiar with their zodiac, or Sun, sign. The twelve signs of the zodiac can also be added to the geomantic chart to provide further information.

Aries

Element: Fire

Ruling planet: Mars

Best day: Tuesday

Aries is the first sign of the zodiac. It is active, enthusiastic, pioneering, and courageous. Arians are natural leaders who have a need to keep busy and active.

The negative side of Aries is impatience, anger, tactlessness, and a tendency to try to do too many things at the same time.

Taurus

Element: Earth

Ruling planet: Venus

Best day: Friday

Taurus is a practical, patient, and goal-oriented sign. It possesses tremendous drive and determination. Taureans are loyal and devoted to their friends. They love beauty and have a strong aesthetic sense.

The negative side of Taurus is obstinacy and stubbornness. They can be inflexible, resentful, and unforgiving.

Gemini

Element: Air

Ruling planet: Mercury

Best day: Wednesday

Gemini is a quick, skillful, ingenious, and versatile sign with an unquenchable desire for knowledge. Geminis learn best in short bursts of activity, rather than sustained periods of concentration. Geminis have a talent with words and make good conversationalists.

The negative side of Gemini is a tendency to start something new without finishing the previous task first. Nervous tension can be a problem.

Cancer

Element: Water

Ruling planet: Moon

Best day: Monday

Cancer is a romantic, emotional, sensitive, feeling, and intuitive sign. Home and family are usually the prime focus of a Cancerian's life. Cancerians are tenacious and usually manage to achieve their goals using their natural charm and people skills.

The negative side of Cancer is fear and a tendency to be easily hurt.

Leo

Element: Fire

Ruling planet: Sun

Best day: Sunday

Leo is ambitious, determined, strong, and enthusiastic. It is also generous, openhearted, and loving. Leos are expansive and like to do everything on a large scale.

The negative side of Leo is pride, along with a tendency to exaggerate.

Virgo

Element: Earth

Ruling planet: Mercury

Best day: Wednesday

Virgo is a modest, down-to-earth, matter-of-fact sign. It is also intelligent, analytical, cautious, and reserved. Virgos constantly aim for perfection and enjoy handling detailed tasks.

The negative side of Virgo is a tendency to be critical.

Libra

Element: Air

Ruling planet: Venus

Best day: Friday

Libra is a harmonious sign with a strong interest in justice and fair play. Librans are diplomatic, tactful, cooperative, cheerful, and loving. They are also considerate, generous, charming, and flexible.

The negative side of Libra is a tendency to be indecisive, superficial, and weak-willed.

Scorpio

Element: Water

Ruling planet: Mars

Best day: Tuesday

Scorpio is a forceful, determined, and tenacious sign. It is secretive, emotional, and intuitive. The major strengths of Scorpio are concentration, imagination, and application.

The negative side of Scorpio is an inability to forgive and forget.

Sagittarius

Element: Fire

Ruling planet: Jupiter

Best day: Thursday

Sagittarius is an enthusiastic, expansive, optimistic, and positive sign. It relates to independence and a philosophical approach to life.

The negative side of Sagittarius is a tendency to dabble.

Capricorn

Element: Earth

Ruling planet: Saturn

Best day: Saturday

Capricorn is a practical, cautious, and patient sign. It is ambitious, and prepared to wait for as long as necessary to achieve its goals.

The negative side of Capricorn is difficulty in expressing emotions and a tendency to be overly serious.

Aquarius

Element: Air

Ruling planet: Saturn

Best day: Saturday

Aquarius is a tolerant, peace-loving, intellectual, and humanitarian sign. Aquarians have a scientific frame of mind and are progressive and sometimes radical with their ideas. They accept others as they are.

The negative side of Aquarius is a tendency to be detached.

Pisces

Element: Water

Ruling planet: Jupiter

Best day: Thursday

Pisces is an imaginative, creative, thoughtful, compassionate, and philanthropic sign.

The negative side of Pisces is a tendency to be overly sensitive and easily hurt.

The Planets

Geomancy uses the Sun, Moon, Mercury, Venus, Jupiter, and Mars, along with the two nodes of the Moon, to create an astrological geomancy chart. These were the traditional "planets" used thousands of years ago. The planets that have been discovered in more recent times are not used in geomancy.

The Sun

Geomancy correspondences: Fortuna Major and Fortuna Minor

Astrological sign: Leo

Astrological houses: First house and tenth house[1]

The Sun is the center of our solar system. In mythology, the Sun has always been considered a wanderer who tirelessly crosses the sky every day. People have always recognized the Sun's life-giving properties, and this is often indicated when artists draw the rays of the Sun that symbolically reach down to touch all living things.

The Sun relates to will, the life force, spirit, power, energy, confidence, vitality, spirit, and organization.

If the qualities of the Sun are used negatively, it creates conceit, egotism, arrogance, and a desire to dominate and control.

The Sun in Aries is progressive, forthright, and ambitious. It is active, courageous, independent, and inclined to be impatient.

The Sun in Taurus is persistent, cautious, and practical. It is also patient, dependable, stable, and conservative.

The Sun in Gemini is sympathetic, restless, and sociable. It is also versatile, adaptable, curious, and changeable.

The Sun in Cancer is sensitive, imaginative, and maternal. It is also tenacious, intuitive, cautious, and nurturing.

The Sun in Leo is active, optimistic, warm, and enthusiastic. It is also passionate, creative, ambitious, and proud.

The Sun in Virgo is modest, thoughtful, conscientious, and responsible. It is also efficient, practical, discriminating, and analytical.

The Sun in Libra is sociable, charming, diplomatic, and harmonious. It is also cooperative, refined, idealistic, and fair.

The Sun in Scorpio is shrewd, penetrating, knowledgeable, and persistent. It is also possessive, secretive, reserved, and calculating.

The Sun in Sagittarius is outgoing, enthusiastic, cheerful, tolerant, and forthright. It is also optimistic, philosophical, expansive, and freedom-loving.

The Sun in Capricorn is cautious, ambitious, responsible, and practical. It is also serious, dependable, conscientious, and economical.

The Sun in Aquarius is unconventional, original, individualistic, and detached. It is also creative, intellectual, idealistic, and forward-looking.

The Sun in Pisces is tolerant, compassionate, imaginative, gentle, creative, and loving. It is also emotional, considerate, self-sacrificing, and kind.

The Moon

Geomancy correspondences: Via and Populus

Astrological sign: Cancer

Astrological houses: Third house (combined with Mercury and Saturn) and ninth house

The Moon reflects light from the Sun. Although ancient astrologers considered it to be a planet, it is a satellite of Earth. The Moon has always been related to fertility, maternal instincts, women, family, domesticity, the subconscious, response, feelings, emotions, and the soul.

If the qualities of the Moon are used negatively, it creates introversion, oversensitivity, moodiness, and a lack of confidence.

The Moon in Aries is emotionally detached, courageous, mentally alert, and ambitious. It is also self-reliant, energetic, impulsive, and independent.

The Moon in Taurus is emotionally stable, faithful, materialistic, and attracted to the very best of everything. It is also determined, resourceful, dependable, and stability-seeking.

The Moon in Gemini is emotionally versatile, logical, creative, and communicative. It is also restless, shrewd, curious, and adaptable.

The Moon in Cancer is sympathetic, clinging, sensitive, intuitive, and family-oriented. It is also peaceful, changeable, emotional, and imaginative.

The Moon in Leo is self-centered, self-reliant, ambitious, honest, and generous. It is also dramatic, warm, and passionate, and it possesses leadership qualities.

The Moon in Virgo is analytical, critical, discriminating, and mentally alert. It is also unassuming, reserved, efficient, and studious.

The Moon in Libra is charming, gracious, refined, affectionate, and appreciative. It is also cooperative, sociable, hospitable, and approval-seeking.

The Moon in Scorpio is impatient, easily hurt, possessive, and dominating. It is also secretive, passionate, emotional, and controlling.

The Moon in Sagittarius is friendly, independent, idealistic, and honest. It is also adventurous, philosophical, aspiring, and eager to learn.

The Moon in Capricorn is sensitive, critical, reserved, and down-to-earth. It is also efficient, serious, reliable, and materialistic.

The Moon in Aquarius is idealistic, emotionally detached, original, and imaginative. It is also sympathetic, independent, unconventional, and inventive.

The Moon in Pisces is intuitive, emotional, affectionate, understanding, and generous. It is also receptive, creative, gentle, and kind.

Mercury

Geomancy correspondences: Conjunctio and Albus

Astrological signs: Gemini and Virgo

Astrological houses: Second house and third house

Mercury is the closest planet to the Sun, and revolves around it once every eighty-eight days. In mythology, Mercury has winged feet and wears a helmet. He also carries a caduceus of entwined snakes. As Mercury is the "Messenger of the Gods," he symbolizes intellect, thought, intelligence, and the conscious mind. Mercury also relates to all forms of communication, self-expression, tact, and diplomacy.

If the qualities of Mercury are used negatively, it creates indecisiveness, nervousness, and an inability to relax.

Mercury in Aries is impetuous, impulsive, and impatient. It is also alert, spontaneous, direct, and original. In this position, Mercury enjoys debates.

Mercury in Taurus is materialistic, determined, stubborn, and cautious. It is also deliberate, practical, and rigid, and it has strong powers of concentration.

Mercury in Gemini is logical, talkative, versatile, and quick to learn. It is also restless, humorous, and unbiased, and it seeks mental stimulation.

Mercury in Cancer is emotional, impressionable, sensitive, and creative. It is also sympathetic, receptive, and tolerant, and it possesses a good memory.

Mercury in Leo is proud, ambitious, optimistic, enthusiastic, and idealistic. It is also dignified, creative, dramatic, and opinionated.

Mercury in Virgo is critical, analytical, impartial, versatile, and logical. It is also accurate, discriminating, cautious, and methodical.

Mercury in Libra is fair, honest, diplomatic, refined, and indecisive. It is also sociable, harmonious, charming, and creative.

Mercury in Scorpio is secretive, shrewd, tenacious, critical, and unforgiving. It is also perceptive, frank, insightful, and sensuous.

Mercury in Sagittarius is generous, sincere, and interested in education, philosophy, and spirituality. It is also independent, tolerant, blunt, and honest.

Mercury in Capricorn is serious, hardworking, methodical, disciplined, and traditional. It is also cautious, ambitious, and a good organizer.

Mercury in Aquarius is original, inventive, independent, scientific, and intuitive. It is also studious, objective, sociable, and curious.

Mercury in Pisces is intuitive, retentive, and sensitive, and it works best in pleasant surroundings. It is also subtle, humorous, imaginative, and creative.

Venus

Geomancy correspondences: Puella and Amissio

Astrological signs: Taurus and Libra

Astrological houses: Fifth house (combined with Saturn and Jupiter) and seventh house

Venus is usually seen only as the morning or evening star. It is described as a cloudy crystal ball, as its gaseous atmosphere is clearly visible from Earth.

In mythology, Venus is the goddess of love. Consequently, Venus relates to love, romance, harmony, gentleness, female sexuality, and physical beauty.

If the qualities of Venus are used negatively, it creates indolence, weakness, procrastination, and sexual addiction.

Venus in Aries is quick-thinking, charismatic, enthusiastic, positive, and cheerful. It is also passionate, demonstrative, idealistic, and impatient.

Venus in Taurus enjoys the best of everything and is sociable, charming, and faithful. It is also patient, sensuous, artistic, and generous.

Venus in Gemini is friendly, mentally stimulating, generous, and freedom-loving. It is also versatile, charming, witty, and refined.

Venus in Cancer seeks security and is sensitive, idealistic, gentle, and charming. It is also sentimental, receptive, sympathetic, and emotional.

Venus in Leo enjoys entertaining and is romantic, loving, proud, and generous. It is also warm, loyal, passionate, and sociable.

Venus in Virgo is analytical, sympathetic, shy, fastidious, and emotionally repressed. It is also discriminating and seeks perfection in all things.

Venus in Libra enjoys beauty in all its forms and is harmonious, sociable, loving, and friendly. It is also popular, charming, diplomatic, and creative.

Venus in Scorpio has deep emotions and is passionate, secretive, intense, and closed. It is also possessive, dominating, mysterious, and intuitive.

Venus in Sagittarius is sociable, outgoing, honest, friendly, and direct. It is also impulsive, loyal, idealistic, and forgiving.

Venus in Capricorn is reserved, repressed, insecure, loyal, and tender. It is also dignified, cautious, conservative, and enduring.

Venus in Aquarius follows its own path and is friendly, detached, and intuitive. It is also idealistic, unselfish, and unconventional.

Venus in Pisces is tender, loving, compassionate, caring, sensitive, and intuitive. It is also impressionable, creative, and empathetic.

Mars

Geomancy correspondences: Puer and Rubeus

Astrological signs: Aries and Scorpio

Astrological house: Sixth house

Mars has a reddish-brown color, as it is comprised largely of aluminium and iron. Because of its color, Mars has always been associated with war. Mars relates to aggression, conflict, energy, assertiveness, and a strong desire for change.

If the qualities of Mars are used negatively, it creates aggressiveness, inconsideration, and recklessness.

Mars in Aries is enthusiastic, independent, courageous, and ambitious. It is also active, energetic, restless, and full of original ideas.

Mars in Taurus is determined, practical, stubborn, cautious, and self-indulgent. It is also earnest, patient, and sensuous.

Mars in Gemini is observant, restless, adventurous, conversational, and mentally alert. It also is persuasive, needs regular stimulation, and enjoys learning.

Mars in Cancer is temperamental, moody, argumentative, and independent. It is also tenacious, sensitive, imaginative, protective, and sympathetic.

Mars in Leo is generous, passionate, demonstrative, confident, enthusiastic, and fun-loving. It is also dramatic, competitive, forceful, and impulsive.

Mars in Virgo enjoys hard work and is disciplined, orderly, logical, and thorough. It is also shrewd, critical, conscientious, and enjoys details.

Mars in Libra is charming, sociable, friendly, and cooperative. It is also popular, refined, passionate, and perceptive.

Mars in Scorpio is honest, self-reliant, disciplined, powerful, incisive, and inflexible. It is also intense, resourceful, relentless, and penetrating.

Mars in Sagittarius is positive, cheerful, optimistic, and full of ideas. It is also enthusiastic, idealistic, adventurous, and impulsive.

Mars in Capricorn is a good organizer that enjoys a challenge. It is disciplined, thoughtful, and practical. It is also ambitious, self-controlled, responsible, and conscientious.

Mars in Aquarius is detached, intellectual, logical, and a natural leader. It is also original, inventive, idealistic, and a natural humanitarian.

Mars in Pisces is sympathetic, sensitive, emotional, and indecisive. It is also warm, affectionate, intuitive, and imaginative.

Jupiter

Geomancy correspondences: Acquisitio and Laetitia

Astrological signs: Sagittarius and Pisces

Astrological houses: Eleventh house and also fifth house (Venus dominant, with Saturn)

The planet Jupiter disappears behind the Sun for one month of every year. Ancient astrologers explained this by saying that he was visiting heaven at this time. In mythology, Jupiter is the King of the Gods, which made him expansive, just, and beneficent. Consequently, Jupiter relates to optimism, abundance, happiness, generosity, reason, justice, and ideas.

If the qualities of Jupiter are used negatively, it creates extravagance, wastefulness, and a tendency to take risks.

Jupiter in Aries has a strong desire for leadership and is enthusiastic, inspirational, and generous. It is also ambitious, confident, philosophical, and sincere.

Jupiter in Taurus is interested in money. It is stubborn and enjoys the best that money can buy. It is also generous, loyal, peaceful, and understanding.

Jupiter in Gemini is original, open-minded, easy to get along with, and full of ideas. It is also restless, curious, humorous, and a good communicator.

Jupiter in Cancer enjoys home and family life. It is sympathetic and good at dealing with people. It is also good-natured, acquisitive, kind, and nurturing.

Jupiter in Leo is positive, enthusiastic, ambitious, and willing to work hard for a specific goal. It is also expansive, generous, dignified, proud, and creative.

Jupiter in Virgo aims high and is analytical, practical, and cooperative. It is also exacting, critical, and conscientious, and it enjoys a challenge.

Jupiter in Libra is conversational, popular, sincere, and nonjudgmental. It is also sociable, diplomatic, fair, and cooperative.

Jupiter in Scorpio is intense, determined, shrewd, and ambitious. It is also resourceful, secretive, controlling, and magnetic.

Jupiter in Sagittarius is generous, sociable, fun-loving, enthusiastic, and ambitious. It is also expansive, sincere, loyal, and good-natured.

Jupiter in Capricorn is honest, honorable, sincere, conservative, ambitious, and cautious. It is also reserved, economical, conscientious, and serious.

Jupiter in Aquarius is tolerant, sociable, original, intellectual, and receptive. It is also outgoing, friendly, cooperative, and intuitive.

Jupiter in Pisces is caring, sympathetic, unassuming, friendly, and compassionate. It is also receptive, kind, idealistic, creative, and intuitive.

Saturn

Geomancy correspondences: Carcer and Tristitia

Astrological signs: Capricorn and Aquarius

Astrological houses: Fifth house and also third house (with the Moon and Mercury)

Until Uranus was discovered in the eighteenth century, Saturn was thought to be the farthest planet from the Sun. Saturn is highly distinctive because of its rings. In mythology, Saturn is related to Chronos, the Greek god of time. Chronos was a bad-tempered god who ate all of his children, except for Zeus—who managed to escape and eventually defeated him. The association with time is an apt one, as it takes Saturn 29½ years to circle the Sun. Saturn relates to limitations, restrictions, patience, organization, seriousness, melancholy, and old age.

If the qualities of Saturn are used negatively, it creates limitation, pessimism, loss, and a self-defeatist state of mind.

Saturn in Aries has a desire for security and is disciplined, inventive, and persistent. It is also acquisitive, self-centered, resourceful, and a good organizer.

Saturn in Taurus desires security and is patient, determined, honest, and practical. It is also reserved, cautious, economical, and stubborn.

Saturn in Gemini is disciplined, logical, intellectual, and studious. It is also resourceful, adaptable, inventive, and observant.

Saturn in Cancer is sensitive, secretive, family-minded, emotional, and responsible. It is also restless, protective, tenacious, and dependant.

Saturn in Leo is cautious, stubborn, mentally alert, confident, and ambitious. It is also responsible, organized, bold, and proud.

Saturn in Virgo is hardworking, practical, cautious, efficient, analytical, and discriminating. It is also orderly, serious, reserved, and exacting.

Saturn in Libra is honest, fair, nonjudgmental, responsible, and patient. It is also impartial, idealistic, and cooperative, and it seeks balance.

Saturn in Scorpio is proud, intense, ambitious, tenacious, and subtle. It is also shrewd, materialistic, insecure, and secretive.

Saturn in Sagittarius is independent, studious, outspoken, and honorable. It is also philosophical, idealistic, honest, and intuitive.

Saturn in Capricorn is persistent, practical, cautious, patient, and ambitious. It is also self-reliant, traditional, serious, and determined.

Saturn in Aquarius is inventive, original, responsible, independent, and freedom-loving. It is also determined, caring, detached, and friendly.

Saturn in Pisces is imaginative, emotional, compassionate, and serious. It is also sensitive, understanding, and lacking in confidence.

The Moon's Nodes

Geomantic correspondences: Caput Draconis and Cauda Draconis

From Earth, the Moon appears to intersect with the ecliptic at two places, 180 degrees apart, called the nodes. When the Moon is heading north, the point where it intersects is called the North Node. Likewise, when the Moon is heading south, the place where it intersects is called the South Node. The North Node brings good fortune, while the South Node indicates bad fortune. The theory behind this is that we all possess both positive and negative qualities. The North Node indicates the good qualities we should develop further. The South Node reveals the less positive characteristics that we are likely to fall back on when placed in a difficult situation.

The Moon's nodes play an important role in Indian astrology. The North Node is called *Rahu*, or the Dragon's Head. This has a strong positive influence and attracts good luck. The South Node is called *Ketu*, or the Dragon's Tail. It is related to negativity and bad luck.

In his 2009 novel *The Lost Symbol*, Dan Brown's protagonist, Robert Langdon, tells a class of students that the cornerstone of the U.S. Capitol building in Washington, DC, was laid between 11:15 a.m. and 12:30 p.m. on September 18, 1793, because at that time Caput Draconis was in the sign of Virgo. A student notes that this might simply be a coincidence. In response, Langdon replies that the cornerstones of the Capitol, the Washington Monument, and the White House—the three structures that comprise the Federal Triangle—were all laid in different years, but all were carefully timed so that Caput Draconis was in Virgo.[2]

The Lost Symbol is fiction, but the information Robert Langdon told his students is fact.[3] The choice of Caput Draconis in Virgo is not surprising when you realize that it relates to spiritual achievement gained through service to others.

Caput Draconis

Caput Draconis in Aries relates to confidence, inner peace, and a desire to follow one's own path.

Caput Draconis in Taurus relates to self-worth, independence, and personal values.

Caput Draconis in Gemini is a sign to think carefully before acting and to focus on one task at a time.

Caput Draconis in Cancer indicates emotional fulfillment gained through working well with others.

Caput Draconis in Leo is a sign to move forward confidently, without worrying about what others may think.

Caput Draconis in Virgo relates to spiritual oneness achieved through service and involvement with others.

Caput Draconis in Libra is a sign that success comes through cooperation with others.

Caput Draconis in Scorpio indicates success through sharing your skills and resources with others.

Caput Draconis in Sagittarius relates to openness, honesty, and learning to trust your intuition.

Caput Draconis in Capricorn relates to self-responsibility and emotional balance.

Caput Draconis in Aquarius relates to success achieved by motivating and appreciating others.

Caput Draconis in Pisces relates to spiritual growth, as well as loving yourself and others.

Cauda Draconis

Cauda Draconis in Aries relates to competitiveness and a desire to win. The lesson comes through learning that true success comes through cooperating with others.

Cauda Draconis in Taurus relates to doing everything singlehandedly, with little or no input from others.

Cauda Draconis in Gemini finds it difficult to make decisions because it is overwhelmed with information.

Cauda Draconis in Cancer indicates looking after others while ignoring one's own concerns.

Cauda Draconis in Leo relates to ego problems and a strong desire to achieve goals, no matter what the cost.

Cauda Draconis in Virgo relates to worry and anxiety when matters do not go as planned.

Cauda Draconis in Libra relates to indecision, fear, codependency, and difficulty in close relationships.

Cauda Draconis in Scorpio relates to accepting other people's beliefs and ideas, instead of developing one's own.

Cauda Draconis in Sagittarius relates to failing to listen to others and believing one is always right.

Cauda Draconis in Capricorn relates to measuring success in material terms, and living through the eyes of others.

Cauda Draconis in Aquarius relates to drifting along with a group, rather than standing on one's own two feet.

Cauda Draconis in Pisces relates to an aversion to the practical side of life by focusing purely on escapism and dreams.

Putting It All Together

Imagine that you own a small business and you're thinking of expansion. You might ask, "Is this a good time to expand my business?"

You create the four Mothers in your usual way. Let's assume you created: Puer, Caput Draconis, Fortuna Minor, and Albus:

First Mother	Second Mother	Third Mother	Fourth Mother
O	O O	O	O O
O	O	O	O O
O O	O	O O	O
O	O	O O	O O
Puer	Caput Draconis	Fortuna Minor	Albus

You create the four Daughters from these:

First Daughter	Second Daughter	Third Daughter	Fourth Daughter
O	O	O O	O
O O	O	O	O
O	O	O O	O O
O O	O O	O	O O
Amisso	Cauda Draconis	Acquisitio	Fortuna Minor

And now the four Nieces:

First Niece	Second Niece	Third Niece	Fourth Niece
O	O	O O	O
O O	O	O	O O
O	O	O O	O O
O O	O O	O O	O
Amisso	Cauda Draconis	Rubeus	Carcer

These create the two Witnesses:

Right Witness	Left Witness
O O	O
O	O
O O	O O
O O	O
Rubeus	Puer

Finally, you create the Judge:

Judge

O

O O

O O

O

Carcer

You can tell right away that this is probably not a good time to expand. Carcer, the Judge, indicates restrictions, limitations, delays, and greed. Rubeus and Puer are also both negative figures. If all you wanted was a quick answer, you could stop at this point. However, as you want your business to grow, you will probably seek more detail.

If this is the case, you continue by placing the Mothers, Daughters, and Nieces in their respective positions on a horoscope chart (see the next page).

The question ("Is this a good time to expand my business?") relates to money, finance, profit, and loss. Consequently, it is a second-house matter.

Caput Draconis is in the second house. Caput Draconis indicates new beginnings, and is especially well placed here, as it usually indicates an improvement in the person's circumstances. However, you need to be careful, as Caput Draconis is favorable when placed with other favorable indicators, but can be negative when placed with unfavorable figures.

Puer is in the first house. As the first house represents you, this is a sign that you may rush into expanding your business without thinking everything through first.

Albus is in house four. This indicates the ultimate outcome. Albus is a positive figure, indicating wisdom and insight. It also indicates slow progress, which puts it at odds with the impulsive Puer.

Let's look at the two Witnesses and the Judge again. Usually, two negative Witnesses and a negative Judge are considered to be bad. However, Carcer could indicate a successful outcome as long as the person remained patient and was willing to accept delays and slow progress. The

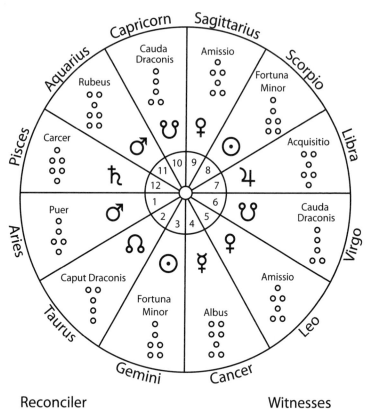

Reconciler

Cauda Draconis

Witnesses

Rubeus   Puer

Judge

Carcer

Chart 6A

person would have to be careful not to be overly greedy or expect too much.

Rubeus, the Right Witness, indicates upheavals, anger, and resentment. However, after experiencing that, if the person is prepared to learn from the experience, he or she will ultimately find the right path.

Puer, the Left Witness, signifies passion, energy, and change. These can be positive attributes. However, Puer often acts without thinking, which makes it a difficult figure to have in this position.

Rubeus indicates the past, Puer the present, and Carcer the future. All of these figures are difficult, but it seems that lessons can be learned and the person will ultimately find the right way forward.

So far, we've examined the houses, Witnesses, and the Judge. Let's add the signs and planets to the reading, and see what extra information they provide.

Puer is the figure in the first house. As Puer relates to Aries, this sign is placed in the first house, and the other signs are placed into the other houses in counterclockwise order. Consequently, Taurus goes into the second house, Gemini into the third, and so on. Pisces, the last sign to be added, goes into the twelfth house. The zodiac signs follow a set order: Aries, Taurus, Gemini, Cancer, Leo, Virgo, Libra, Scorpio, Sagittarius, Capricorn, Aquarius, Pisces.

Each figure relates to a specific planet, and these are placed in the houses that relate to the particular figures. For the sake of convenience, here are the planets and the figures they relate to:

Sun: Fortuna Major, Fortuna Minor

Moon: Via, Populus

Mercury: Conjunctio, Albus

Venus: Puella, Amissio

Mars: Puer, Rubeus

Jupiter: Acquisitio, Laetitia

Saturn: Carcer, Tristitia

Moon's North Node: Caput Draconis

Moon's South Node: Cauda Draconis

Puer, the figure in the first house, relates to the planet Mars. Because of this, we place Mars inside the first house.

We continue working our way around the chart. Caput Draconis in the second house relates to (and in fact is) the Moon's North Node. Consequently, this is placed in the second house.

Fortuna Minor appears in houses three and eight. Consequently, the Sun is placed in both of these houses. This is a major difference from traditional astrology. All the planets appear just once in a standard horoscope. However, they can appear a number of times in a geomantic astrology chart.

Albus, in the fourth house, relates to Mercury, which is placed in this position.

Amissio, which relates to Venus, is in houses five and nine. Consequently, Venus is placed in both houses.

Cauda Draconis is found in houses six and ten. Consequently, the Moon's South Node is placed in both of these houses.

Jupiter, which relates to Acquisitio, is placed in house seven.

Mars, which relates to Rubeus, is placed in house eleven.

Saturn, which relates to Carcer, is placed in the twelfth house, and completes the placement of the planets.

Now we can look at the question again, using the added information provided by the planets and zodiac signs. The question is, "Is this a good time to expand my business?"

Mars and Puer are both in the first house. Puer is at its strongest in the first house, and also happens to be the planetary ruler of Aries. Mars encourages you to rush in too quickly.

Caput Draconis and the Moon's North Node are in the second house. This is a positive indication that the expansion will bring financial reward.

To see how the question will be concluded, we look at Albus and Mercury, which are in the fourth house. Albus indicates slow but steady progress. Mercury indicates a great deal of communication and thought.

Finally, we look at the Judge, which is Carcer. This indicates limitations, restrictions, delays, and possible greed. It almost always indicates a negative outcome, and in financial matters it can indicate major setbacks.

Carcer also appears in house twelve. This is the house of secret enemies, dangers, restrictions, and sorrows. This is not a good sign, as it indicates that factors you are not aware of will work against you. Saturn in Pisces is imaginative, serious, compassionate, and lacking in confidence.

This indicates that timidity and an overactive imagination will prevent you from taking active steps to expand the business.

Consequently, this chart creates an interesting mix of both favorable and unfavorable possibilities. To help decide whether or not to proceed with the plans for expansion, you can create a Reconciler using the Judge and Caput Draconis (the figure in house two). This creates Cauda Draconis. Cauda Draconis represents endings, which means it is a favorable figure for anything that is nearing completion but is unfavorable for anything else. As the question relates to expansion, Cauda Draconis in this position indicates a negative outcome.

Part of Fortune

As this question ultimately relates to money, you can also determine where the Part of Fortune is located in the chart. This might give some indication as to where the money will come from. The Part of Fortune is determined by adding up all the points of the Mothers, Daughters, and Nieces, and dividing the total by 12. The remainder, rather than the answer, tells you the house that the Part of Fortune is located in. If there is no remainder, the Part of Fortune is placed in the twelfth house.

There are 69 points in the figures in chart 6A. These are the Mothers, Daughters, and Nieces. The number 69 divided by 12 is 5, with a remainder of 9. Consequently, for this reading the Part of Fortune is in the ninth house. This house relates to extensive travel and dealings with foreigners. It contains Amissio, indicating a loss. In this divination, the Part of Fortune is another indication that it is not a good time to try to expand the business.

Considering the chart as a whole, it looks as if you should continue planning, but recognize that this is not a good time to attempt to expand your business. If, despite this warning, you do try to expand, you'll need to be cautious and extremely brave. You will also need to prepare each move carefully before proceeding. The main impediment to progress is likely to be you. If you're able to keep your impulsiveness under control, your business will do well.

In this example, the figures in the first house (indicating the questioner) and the house that related to the question are different. If the two figures happen to be the same, they effectively answer the question. If the two figures are favorable ones, the questioner will be extremely happy with the outcome. If the two figures are unfavorable, the questioner will be happy initially but may regret the outcome later.

Aspects

Aspects are the relationships between the different planets in the chart. In astrology charts these can be measured precisely, but this is not possible in a geomantic astrology chart. The aspects that relate to the first house (the questioner) and the house that relates to the question are not read. Caput Draconis and Cauda Draconis do not form aspects with other planets. The other difference is that not all the aspects used in an astrology chart are used in a geomantic chart. Conversely, geomantic astrology includes an aspect that is not used in traditional astrology. This is when an aspect occurs between two adjacent houses. (There is an aspect in traditional astrology known as a Conjunction. This occurs when two planets are situated less that eight degrees from each other. Sometimes these two planets are in different houses, making this similar to the geomantic aspect between two houses.)

The astrological aspects that are interpreted in a geomantic chart are called the *trine, square,* and *sextile.*

Trine

A trine aspect is considered favorable. It creates a gentle, stress-free relationship between the two houses. It helps otherwise negative charts by offering hope that the situation will improve. A trine is created when two planets are situated 120 degrees, or four houses, away from each other.

Square

A square aspect is unfavorable, as it creates frustration and discord between the two figures. A square aspect can be considered a major learning experience. A square is created when two planets are situated 90 degrees, or three houses, apart.

Sextile

A sextile aspect is considered favorable. It brings thought, communication, and creative ideas into the question. A sextile aspect is created when two planets are situated 60 degrees, or two houses, apart.

Aspects are created when the same figure appears in two houses that are in aspect to each other. If Via, for instance, were found in both the second and fourth houses, it creates a sextile aspect. Likewise, if a particular figure appeared in both the fourth and seventh houses, it would create a square aspect. A trine aspect would be created if a particular planet appeared in, for example, both house three and house seven.

However, the aspects can sometimes be more complicated than this. There are occasions when different figures are ruled by the same planet. These also become aspects. Here are the figures that create this possibility:

Sun figures: Fortuna Major and Fortuna Minor

Moon figures: Via and Populus

Mercury figures: Conjunctio and Albus

Venus figures: Puella and Amissio

Mars figures: Puer and Rubeus

Saturn figures: Carcer and Tristitia

In geomancy, there is also a specific aspect between certain pairs of houses that does not apply in traditional astrology. The first and second houses can be paired, as can houses three and four, five and six, seven and eight, nine and ten, and eleven and twelve. These are known as *companion houses*. However, there is no aspect between houses two and three, four and five, six and seven, eight and nine, ten and eleven, and twelve and one. Consequently, they are not companion houses.

Companion houses are created in one of three ways:

1. When the same figure appears in both houses.

2. When both houses contain figures ruled by the same planet.

3. When the two houses contain opposite figures. The opposite figures are: Fortuna Major and Fortuna Minor, Via and Populus, Puella and Puer, Acquisitio and Amissio, Conjunctio and Carcer, Tristitia and Laetitia, Albus and Rubeus, and Caput Draconis and Cauda Draconis.

Summary of the Process

1. Think of your question.

2. Cast the four Mothers, and create the remaining figures, including the two Witnesses and the Judge.

3. Look at the Witnesses and the Judge to determine if they are favorable or unfavorable.

4. Place the first twelve figures in their respective houses.

5. Look at the figure in the first house. Traditionally, if Rubeus or Cauda Draconis were in this position, the chart was destroyed. It was thought that Rubeus in the first house meant that the person asking the question was not being completely honest with the geomancer. If Cauda Draconis was in this position, it meant that the person asking the question had already decided what to do, making any reading superfluous. You have three possibilities when this occurs. You may destroy the chart. You might tell the person asking for the reading what the figure means in this position, and try to ascertain his or her motives before proceeding. Alternatively, you might read the chart, but be careful with what you

say. If this occurs when you are preparing a chart for yourself, pause and think about your reasons for asking this particular question.

6. Add the planets and the zodiac signs.

7. Determine which house applies to your question and examine the figure, planet, and zodiac sign.

8. Check to see if this figure appears anywhere else in the chart. If it does, think about the qualities of the house it is in to see if it affects the answer. Determine if the two figures create an aspect to each other.

9. Examine the figure, planet, and zodiac sign in the first house. Again, check to see if this figure appears elsewhere in the chart.

10. Examine the figure, planet, and zodiac sign in the fourth house to determine the final outcome. Check to see if this figure appears elsewhere.

11. Look for any companion houses.

12. Check to see if the figure of the Judge appears anywhere else in the chart. The house or houses it appears in will have a powerful effect on the outcome.

13. If the outcome is still unclear, you can create a Reconciler figure using the points of the Judge and the figure in the house that relates to the question.

14. If the question relates to money, determine the Part of Fortune to see where the money is likely to come from.

Asking Questions for Others

Everything we have covered so far assumes that you are the person asking the question and the answer concerns you, or that you have constructed a chart for someone to answer a question that relates mainly to him or her. However, once people discover your interest in geomancy, they will want you to answer questions relating to other people. The normal rules apply if the person's question relates to his or her relationship with someone else. However, if the question involves matters relating to someone else's life, the house that relates to the person most involved in the divination is considered to be the first house. Only the houses that relate to specific people are used. Consequently, if the person asks a question about his or her brother, for instance, the third house would be considered the first house. Here is the list of possibilities:

Third house: Person's brothers, sisters, and neighbors.

Fourth house: Person's father.

Fifth house: Person's children, plus any sexual partners the person may have outside of his or her main relationship.

Sixth house: Person's employees, as well as his or her pets and small animals, such as a cat or dog.

Seventh house: Person's partner, lover, business associates, known enemies, and people with whom he or she has no personal association.

Ninth house: Person's teachers and mentors.

Tenth house: Person's mother, as well as people who hold authority over him or her, such as an employer or judge.

Eleventh house: Person's friends, associates, co-workers, traveling companions, stepchildren, and adopted children.

Twelfth house: Unknown enemies and large animals, such as a horse or cow owned by the person.

In addition to this, the house that is the subject of the question is also moved in a counterclockwise direction. Consequently, if the question related to the person's brother (third house), and whether this was a good time for him to propose marriage, you would not look at the seventh house (marriage and partnerships) as you would if you were asking the question for yourself. Instead, you would count seven houses from the house that relates to the person the question is being asked about, starting from, in this example, house three. (Three, four, five, six, seven, eight, nine.) Consequently, you'd look at the ninth house.

A number of variations of astrological geomancy have been devised over the years. The two most important of these were the methods created by Gerard of Cremona and Cornelius Agrippa. We will look at them in the next two chapters.

seven

Gerard of Cremona

Gerard of Cremona (c. 1114–87) was born in Cremona in Lombardy, Italy. At some point before the year 1144, he traveled to Toledo in Spain to learn Arabic, as he wanted to read *Almagest*, a book by Ptolemy, the second-century astronomer, that had not been translated into Latin. Gerard ultimately translated this book, and it became a valuable textbook for astronomers and astrologers for some three hundred years.

Gerard spent the rest of his life in Toledo, and is said to have translated at least eighty manuscripts from Arabic into Latin. These included a number of Greek authors whose work had been translated into Arabic, but not Latin. They included Aristotle, the philosopher; Euclid, the mathematician; and Galen, the physician. His most famous translation was the *Canon* by Avicenna, a tenth-century Persian physician. It is not known if Gerard was personally responsible for all of these translations, as the name of the translator was not always included in early printed editions. It's possible that he headed a school of translators and supervised many of the translations attributed to him, rather than personally translating them all.

Consequently, it's impossible to tell if the method of astrological geomancy attributed to Gerard of Cremona is his original creation, or if it's a translation from an Arabic work. No matter where it came from, it's a fascinating variation that many people have used over the centuries and still use today.

The basics of Gerard's system are simpler than the methods we have already discussed. However, to use his system effectively it is helpful to have a reasonable knowledge of astrology to interpret the horoscope chart.

Once again, you start by thinking of your question. Once you have this question firmly in your mind, you construct a geomantic figure. This must be done by making four lines of marks on the ground or on a sheet of paper. Make each row of marks in a right-to-left order. As you know, an odd number of marks creates a single dot, and an even row creates two dots. This figure goes into the first house (see chart 7A).

Let's assume your question is, "Shall I visit my brother in the UK this year?" You make four rows of dots on a sheet of paper and create Albus:

○ ○ (16 dots) ....

○ ○ (14 dots) ....

○ (11 dots) ....

○ ○ (14 dots) ....

The second step is to relate this figure to an astrological sign. Gerard devised his own list of associations:

Puer: Gemini

Amissio: Scorpio

Albus: Cancer

Populus: Capricorn

Via: Leo

Fortuna Major: Aquarius

Fortuna Minor: Taurus

Conjunctio: Virgo

Puella: Libra

Rubeus: Gemini

Acquisitio: Aries

Carcer: Pisces

Tristitia: Scorpio

Laetitia: Taurus

Caput Draconis: Virgo

Cauda Draconis: Sagittarius

As Albus is associated with the sign of Cancer, Cancer is placed in the first house. The other signs are then placed into each house in the usual order (Aries, Taurus, Gemini,

Cancer, Leo, Virgo, Libra, Scorpio, Sagittarius, Capricorn, Aquarius, and Pisces). Consequently, Leo is placed in house two, Virgo in house three, and so on.

The third step is to insert the planets into their correct houses. This is done by creating four rows of dots for each planet. The total of all the dots is divided by 12, and the remainder indicates which house the particular planet is to go into. If there is no remainder, the planet goes into the twelfth house.

The "planets" need to be worked out in a specific order: Sun, Moon, Venus, Mercury, Saturn, Jupiter, Mars, and Caput Draconis.

Let's assume that for the Sun you created:

(18 dots) . . . .
(13 dots)   . . . .
(16 dots)   . . . .
(19 dots) . . . .

18 + 13 + 16 + 19 = 66. The number 66 divided by 12 = 5, with a 6 remainder. Consequently, the Sun is placed in the sixth house.

You make four rows of dots again to determine which house the Moon is to go in. After doing the math, the remainder is 3. This means the Moon goes into the third house. You use the same process for the other planets and find that:

Venus goes into the seventh house
Mercury goes into the third house

Saturn goes into the twelfth house
Jupiter goes into the first house
Mars goes into the ninth house
Caput Draconis goes into the fifth house

The Moon's Nodes are always 180 degrees apart. Consequently, as Caput Draconis is in the fifth house, Cauda Draconis is placed directly opposite in the eleventh house.

In this system of astrological geomancy, it is possible for more than one planet to be in the same house. In this example, the Moon and Mercury are both in the third house.

The chart is now complete, and is ready to be interpreted (see chart 7A on the next page).

The first house relates to Jupiter and the sign of Cancer. Jupiter relates to optimism, expansion, and ideas. Cancer is emotional and sensitive. It relates strongly to home and family. It's not surprising that you're considering a trip to visit your brother this year. Your question concerns both travel and family. Travel is a ninth-house matter. We have Mars and the sign of Pisces in the ninth house. Mars is assertive and indicates a strong desire for change. However, it also relates to disagreements and conflict. Pisces is gentle, compassionate, and easily hurt. If Mars is able to listen to the intuitive nature of Pisces, you will come up with many creative ideas. Even so, if you take this trip, you might find yourself participating in a family argument or disagreement of some sort.

Siblings relate to the third house. In this position you have the Moon, Mercury, and the sign of Virgo. The Moon relates to home and family. In Virgo, the Moon is inclined

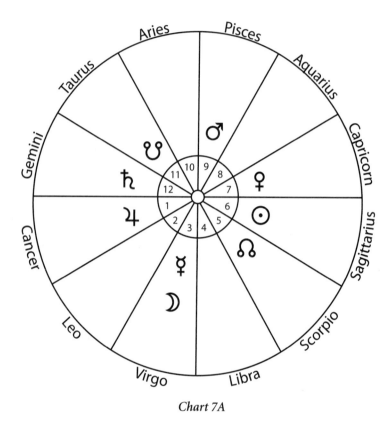

Chart 7A

to be down-to-earth and practical. Mercury relates to communication, as well as tact and diplomacy. Virgo is cautious and reserved, but has a tendency to be critical. You will probably have to make an effort to be uncritical, tactful, and kind while visiting your brother.

House four indicates the outcome. There are no planets in this house. However, it relates to Libra, which is harmonious, easy to get along with, and fair.

It looks as if you should take the trip this year. You'll have a good time, but you might need to make a special effort to avoid any family squabbles or disagreements.

As you can see, in Gerard's system no geomantic figures appear in the chart; each planet appears only once; and Caput Draconis and Cauda Draconis are correctly placed 180 degrees apart. Because of this, Gerard's system is much more likely to appeal to traditional astrologers than the other systems of geomantic astrology.

Several years ago, a friend asked me to create a geomancy chart for her. She had been involved in astrology for most of her life, but had never explored geomancy. She was curious about it, though, and asked me to use geomancy to answer a question for her. Her question was, "Is it a good idea for me to take up astrology as a career?" I could have constructed a geomantic chart using any of the methods in this book, but because of her interest in astrology, it made sense to use the method devised by Gerard of Cremona.

I made four rows of dots, which created Fortuna Major:

    O O .... (14 dots)

    O O .... (16 dots)

       O .... (15 dots)

       O .... (17 dots)

As Fortuna Major relates to the sign of Aquarius, I placed it as the Ascendant (in the first house), and followed it with Pisces in the second house, Aries in the third, and so on, until I finished with Capricorn in the twelfth house (chart 7B).

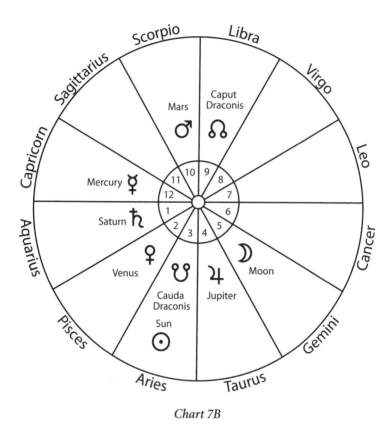

Chart 7B

I created four rows of dots for each planet, divided the total by 12, and using the remainder I found that:

The Sun was in the third house

The Moon was in the fifth house

Venus was in the second house

Mercury was in the twelfth house

Saturn was in the first house

Jupiter was in the fourth house

Mars was in the tenth house

Caput Draconis was in the ninth house

I placed the planets into their respective houses. Cauda Draconis went into the third house, directly opposite Caput Draconis in the ninth house. The chart was now complete, and could be interpreted.

The first house deals with the person asking the question. Aquarius, as ruler of the first house, is outgoing, sociable, and intuitive. Saturn in Aquarius tends to slow everything down. It relates to caution, limitations, patience, and perseverance. It shows that my friend will not act impulsively, but once a decision has been made, will work towards her goal with persistence and tenacity. Saturn in Aquarius also shows my friend would be a good, patient researcher, especially in scientific pursuits.

The second house relates to my friend's possessions, as well as her ability at making money. Pisces rules the second house. Pisces is sensitive, mystical, and emotional. The sensitivity and creative potential of Venus are enhanced by its placement in this position.

The tenth house is the house of career. Scorpio rules my friend's tenth house. Mars in Scorpio is an extremely good combination, as it shows that the energy produced by Mars will be expressed with enormous intensity and drive. This gives a strong desire to succeed.

The fourth house indicates the outcome. In this position we have Jupiter in Taurus. This shows that my friend will do well in her chosen career. She will experience happiness, abundance, and satisfaction working as an astrologer.

My friend watched me draw up the chart and was excited when I told her the good news. All the same, she was cautious, and two years passed before she gave up her regular job and became a full-time astrologer. It took her several months to become established, and in her first year she made significantly less money than she would have in her previous job. However, her income increased dramatically the following year, and she is now kept extremely busy preparing charts, teaching astrology, and writing newspaper articles on the subject. She is also happier than she's ever been before, as she's following her passion.

In the next chapter, we'll look at how Cornelius Agrippa did his geomancy readings.

eight

Cornelius Agrippa

Henry Cornelius Agrippa von Nettesheim (1486–1535) was arguably the most important occultist of the Renaissance. He was also an accomplished soldier, writer, and physician. He was well-educated and could speak eight languages fluently. Throughout his life he traveled widely throughout Europe, spending periods of time in Italy, France, Switzerland, England, and Belgium. His *Three Books of Occult Philosophy*, written between 1509 and 1510, had a huge influence on generations of occultists and is still an essential book for anyone interested in the subject today.[1] Agrippa was concerned about the ramifications if his *Occult Philosophy* were to be published, and sent a copy to Abbot Johannes Trithemius (1462–1516), the German humanist and occult scholar, asking for his views.

Abbot Trithemius was a good choice. As well as being a highly respected author of books on theology and humanism, he had written a book called *Steganographia*, which included what were considered to be magical invocations. In fact, the book was a text on steganography, the art of secret communication. However, the scandal and difficulties it created forced Abbot Trithemius to hide it.

Abbot Trithemius was enthusiastic about Agrippa's book, but sent him a warning letter. Trithemius wrote that Agrippa should "communicate vulgar secrets to vulgar friends, but higher and secret to higher and secret friends only . . . lest you be trod under the oxen's feet."[2]

Cornelius Agrippa devised his own system of geomancy, which was published in English as *Of Geomancy* in *Henry Cornelius Agrippa, His Fourth Book of Occult Philosophy*. Although this book is a forgery, the section on geomancy appears to be genuine.[3]

Although Agrippa knew a great deal about geomancy, he seems to have had mixed feelings on the subject. After mentioning works by Haly, Gerard of Cremona, Bartholomew of Parma, and Tundinus, he wrote: "I too have written a geomancy quite different from the rest but no less superstitious and fallacious or if you wish I will even say 'mendacious.'"[4] However, as Agrippa was always considered a somewhat suspect character, he may have written this to protect himself from charges of witchcraft. It's also possible that, even though he may have had doubts about the veracity of geomancy, it didn't prevent him from practicing the art.

Agrippa believed that geomancy worked because the strong desire of the person asking the question influenced the choice of figures used in the reading. He related the traditional Mothers and Daughters to the planets in the usual way. The Nieces were created separately, using a method he devised. The Nieces also related to the usual planets. Interestingly, Agrippa did not name the figures that derived from the *Matres* (Mothers) and *Filiae* (Daughters). For the sake of convenience, we'll continue to call them the Nieces.

Agrippa used a different system of relating each figure to a sign of the zodiac. In his system:

Carcer relates to Capricorn

Tristitia relates to Aquarius

Acquisitio relates to Pisces

Laetitia relates to Sagittarius

Puer relates to Aries

Rubeus relates to Scorpio

Fortuna Major relates to Leo

Fortuna Minor relates to Leo

Puella relates to Taurus

Amissio relates to Libra

Conjunctio relates to Virgo

Albus relates to Gemini

Via relates to Cancer

Populus relates to Cancer

Caput Draconis relates to Capricorn

Cauda Draconis relates to Scorpio

The figures, and the planets that relate to them, are placed into the twelve houses of the zodiac in a different order from the method we have already discussed. In our earlier example, the four Mothers were placed into houses one to four, the four Daughters into houses five to eight, and the four Nieces into houses nine to twelve.

In Agrippa's system, the first Mother is placed in the first house. The second Mother is placed in the tenth house, the third Mother in the seventh house, and the fourth Mother in the fourth house. As you can see, the Mothers are placed into the horoscope in a clockwise direction. If you visualize the astrological chart as a clock, the four Mothers are between eight and nine o'clock (first Mother in house one), eleven and twelve o'clock (second Mother in house ten), two and three o'clock (third Mother in house seven), and five and six o'clock (fourth Mother in house four).

The Daughters are placed into the houses in the same way. The first Daughter goes into house two, the second Daughter into house eleven, the third Daughter into house eight, and the fourth Daughter into house five.

This leaves four positions for the Nieces. These are constructed in a totally different way that appears to have been invented by Agrippa, who used the elemental triplicities of astrology to create the Nieces. The trines divide the twelve houses into four groups of three, 120 degrees apart. By doing this, Agrippa ensured that the Mothers, Daughters, and Nieces have a figure in all four of the elements: Fire, Earth, Air, and Water.

Houses one, five, and nine create a triangle (element of Fire), as do houses two, six, and ten (element of Earth); houses three, seven, and eleven (element of Air); and houses four, eight, and twelve (element of Water). In these triangles, the Nieces appear in houses three, six, nine, and twelve. They are created from the Mother and Daughter that belong inside the same triangle. This means that the Niece in house three, for instance, is created from the Mother in house seven and the Daughter in house eleven. Consequently, if the Mother were Acquisitio and the Daughter Puer, the Niece would be Laetitia:

Mother	Daughter	Niece
O O	O	O
O	O	O O
O O	O O	O O
O	O	O O
Acquisitio	Puer	Laetitia

Once the twelve figures have been placed in position, the planets that relate to them are placed into the houses. Finally, the astrological sign that relates to the figure is placed beside house one, and the other signs are placed into position in a counterclockwise order. Let's assume we've constructed a chart, and Laetitia is the figure in the first house. In Agrippa's system, Laetitia relates to Sagittarius. This means that Sagittarius relates to house one, Capricorn to house two, Aquarius to house three, and so on, until we finish with Scorpio in house twelve.

Cornelius Agrippa used the traditional Witnesses and the Judge when performing shield geomancy. However, when he performed astrological geomancy, he created the Judge, which he called the Index, in an unusual way. The

Index was determined by adding up all the dots that were used when creating the Mothers. These are not the number of dots that make up the figures, but the number of dots made on a sheet of paper, or holes made in sand, to generate the figures in the first place. This total is divided by 12. If there is no remainder, the Index (or Judge) is the figure in house twelve. If there is a remainder, the houses are counted in a counterclockwise direction, starting from the first house. This means that if the remainder were four, the Index would be the figure in the fourth house. In practice, it's simpler to remember that the house number is the same number as the remainder. If the remainder were seven, for instance, the Index would be the figure in the seventh house.

The chart is now complete and can be interpreted in the usual way. The first house represents the person asking the question, a particular house relates to the person's concern, and house four indicates the outcome. If the result is unclear, the Index is used to clarify the situation. Agrippa wrote about the Index: "But if on either part they shall be equal, or ambiguous, then the Index alone shall certify you of the thing quesited."[5]

Example

Let's assume your question is, "How will my relationship with [my girlfriend or boyfriend] develop over the next three months?" You create the Mothers by making marks, in the manner described in chapter 1, on a sheet of paper or on the ground. This produces:

First Mother

(18 marks) ○ ○
(15 marks) ○
(16 marks) ○ ○
(17 marks) ○

Acquisitio

Second Mother

(15 marks) ○
(16 marks) ○ ○
(18 marks) ○ ○
(16 marks) ○ ○

Laetitia

Third Mother

(15 marks) ○
(15 marks) ○
(18 marks) ○ ○
(17 marks) ○

Puer

Fourth Mother

(16 marks) ○ ○
(17 marks) ○
(15 marks) ○
(15 marks) ○

Caput Draconis

From these, you produce the four Daughters:

First Daughter

○ ○
○
○
○ ○

Conjunctio

Second Daughter

○
○ ○
○
○

Puella

Third Daughter

○ ○
○ ○
○ ○
○

Tristitia

Fourth Daughter

○
○ ○
○
○

Puella

The Mothers and Daughters are placed in the chart (8A). The first Mother goes into the first house, the second into the tenth house, the third into the seventh house, and the fourth into the fourth house.

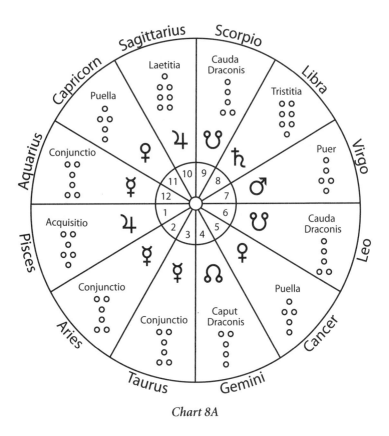

Chart 8A

The first Daughter goes into the second house, the second into the eleventh house, the third into the eighth house, and the fourth into the fifth house.

The four Nieces are created using the method Agrippa devised. Consequently, the figure in the ninth house is created from the figures in the first and fifth houses:

House One	+	House Five	produces	House Nine
O O		O		O
O		O O		O
O O		O		O
O		O		O O

House Two	+	House Ten	produces	House Six
O O		O		O
O		O O		O
O		O O		O
O O		O O		O O

House Seven	+	House Eleven	produces	House Three
O		O		O O
O		O O		O
O O		O		O
O		O		O O

House Four	+	House Eight	produces	House Twelve
O O		O O		O O
O		O O		O
O		O O		O
O		O		O O

This places a figure in each of the twelve houses. The next step is to insert the planets that relate to each figure and to enter the zodiac signs beside each house. Using Agrippa's system, Acquisitio, the figure in the first house, relates to Pisces. Consequently, Pisces is written beside house one, Aries beside house two, Taurus beside house three, and so on. Aquarius, the final zodiac sign to be entered, goes beside house twelve.

The final step is to determine the Index, or Judge. This is worked out by adding up the number of marks generated to produce the four Mothers, dividing the result by 12, and seeing what the remainder is. In this example, the total is 259, which, divided by 12 gives us 21, with a remainder of 7. This means the Index is in the seventh house.

The chart is now complete, and you can examine it to find an answer to your question. In this example, the question is: "How will my relationship with [my girlfriend/boyfriend] develop over the next three months?"

You have Pisces, Acquisitio, and Jupiter in the first house. Pisces is imaginative, dreamy, compassionate, thoughtful, and giving. Jupiter is optimistic, generous, happy, and positive. When Jupiter is in Pisces, it is also caring, sympathetic, compassionate, and friendly. Acquisitio indicates success, and indicates that whatever you desire is within reach.

The house that specifically relates to your question is the seventh house, the house of partnerships and close relationships. In this position we have Virgo, Puer, and Mars. Virgo is modest, down-to-earth, intelligent, and reserved. Mars is forceful, assertive, and dynamic. Mars in Virgo enjoys hard work and challenges, and uses a disciplined approach. Puer represents passion, energy, and sudden change. It is highly charged, sexually.

Puer is also the Index figure, and you can examine that, if the rest of the chart gives you an inconclusive answer. Cornelius Agrippa wrote: "That figure [in the house indicated by the Index] giveth you a competent judgement of the thing quesited; and this together with the significations of the judgements aforesaid. But if on either part they shall be equal, or ambiguous, then the Index alone shall certify you of the thing quesited."[6]

The fourth house, indicating the outcome, contains Gemini, Caput Draconis, and the Moon's North Node. Gemini is a quick, versatile, and active sign. It indicates communication, especially through conversation. Caput Draconis is a positive sign that helps matters to grow and develop. It often indicates a successful result after a slow or difficult start. Caput Draconis in Gemini is a sign that you should think carefully before acting.

All of this is positive and shows that the relationship is likely to develop over the next three months. Your goal is within reach, and you should be feeling enthusiastic, passionate, and optimistic. Caput Draconis in the fourth house indicates success. If there was any doubt, Puer, the Index figure, provides passion and energy, both positive factors in helping a relationship to develop.

As you can see, the system devised by Cornelius Agrippa is useful and highly practical. The major disadvantage is that individual planets can appear several times in a chart, creating major confusion when trying to interpret the aspects accurately. Because of this, most people who have studied astrology prefer the methods of Gerard of Cremona.

After Agrippa, there were no major developments in geomancy until the late nineteenth century, when the Hermetic Order of the Golden Dawn included a version of it in their courses. We will look at their methods in the next chapter.

nine

The Hermetic Order
of the Golden Dawn

In 1886, William Wynn Westcott, a London coroner and occultist, was browsing in a bookseller's stall when he came across a set of mysterious documents written in code. Once decoded, the documents were found to contain the outlines of a course taught by a magical order called the Hermetic Order of the Golden Dawn. Fortunately, the name and address of a Rosicrucian adept in Germany, Anna Sprengel, was included with the papers. Westcott wrote to her, and received permission to amplify the outlines and set up a magical order. Unfortunately, Sprengel died immediately after this, but the letter she wrote to Westcott is still in existence. However, this letter was obviously written by someone who did not know much German, and this fact, along with a number of other discrepancies, makes the whole story suspect.

However, there is no doubt whatsoever that, in March 1888, Westcott, Samuel Liddell Mathers, and William Robert Woodman founded the Hermetic Order of the Golden Dawn. Initially, the members were all friends and associates of the founders, but membership gradually increased. At one stage, the order had more than one hundred members, including William Butler Yeats, Algernon Blackwood, Arthur Machen, Arthur Edward Waite, Evelyn Underhill, Aleister Crowley, Dion Fortune, and Israel Regardie. Years later, Regardie wrote a series of books about the Golden Dawn, thereby ensuring that their teachings survived. In fact, there are more people studying and practicing the Golden Dawn system of magic today than ever before.

Initially, the order offered five grades, or levels, to its members. Geomancy was taught at the Zelator, or second, grade.

The students were taught several ways to construct the sixteen figures. These included making dots on a sheet of paper, making marks on the ground, counting handfuls of pebbles, rolling dice, and tossing coins. The recommended method was to fill a box with earth and use a stick to make marks on the surface.

The Hermetic Order of the Golden Dawn was a magical order focused on ceremonial magic. Not surprisingly, they created a ritual around the process of constructing geomantic charts. Before generating the figures, the person doing the reading needs to choose a geomantic spirit, called a *Genius*. The *Genii* are the ruling spirits of the planetary energies that are invoked during the reading. In a sense, they are the souls of the planets they represent. They are derived from the planets that rule each of the geomantic figures. As the choice of question determines which Genius is the best one to use, the question has to be clearly formulated before choosing a Genius. The success of the reading depends entirely on the person's ability at invoking the desired Genius, or spirit.

Here are the sixteen figures, with the genii that relate to them:

Figure	Planet	Genius
Puer	Mars	Bartzabel
Amissio	Venus	Kedemel
Albus	Mercury	Taphthartharath
Populus	Moon	Chasmodai
Via	Moon	Chasmodai
Fortuna Major	Sun	Sorath
Fortuna Minor	Sun	Sorath
Conjunctio	Mercury	Taphthartharath
Puella	Venus	Kedemel
Rubeus	Mars	Bartzabel
Acquisitio	Jupiter	Hismael
Carcer	Saturn	Zazel
Tristitia	Saturn	Zazel
Laetitia	Jupiter	Hismael
Caput Draconis	Venus and Jupiter	Hismael and Kedemel
Cauda Draconis	Mars and Saturn	Zazel and Bartzabel

These spirits were not invented by the Golden Dawn, but they are part of the lore of ceremonial magic and are mentioned in Cornelius Agrippa's *Three Books of Occult Philosophy*. Their origin is unknown, but they predate Agrippa and are known as the Hebrew Spirits of the Planets. The symbolism attached to each spirit includes gender, an element, planet, colors, direction, and the spirit's area of interest.

Because the genii, or spirits, have no concept of ethics or responsibility, when left alone they'll use the powers of the planets associated with them in a random and uncontrolled manner. This is potentially dangerous, which is why the genii are always summoned and released using the name of their intelligences, as well as the names of the gods, goddesses, or angels that relate to their planets.

Zazel

Gender: Male

Element: Earth

Planet: Saturn

Intelligence: Agiel

Colors: Sapphire blue and black

Direction: East

Zazel is reserved, thoughtful, and silent. He governs time, death, agriculture, philosophy, and history. He gets along well with Taphthartharath, but all the other spirits consider him an enemy.

Hismael

Gender: Male

Element: Air

Planet: Jupiter

Intelligence: Iophiel

Colors: Sea green, violet, and gray

Direction: Northeast

Hismael is peaceful, calm, and easygoing. He governs good fortune, growth and development, charities and benevolent institutions, entertainment, and upward progress, especially advancement in one's career. Hismael gets along well with Chasmodai, Kedemel, Sorath, and Taphthartharath, but Bartzabel and Zazel consider him an enemy.

Bartzabel

Gender: Male

Element: Fire

Planet: Mars

Intelligence: Graphiel

Colors: Red and yellow

Direction: West

Bartzabel is enthusiastic, passionate, and impulsive. He rules conflicts and disputes, surgery, male sexuality, and all animals. He gets along well with Kedemel and Sorath, but is considered an enemy by Chasmodai, Hismael, Taphthartharath, and Zazel.

Sorath

Gender: Male

Element: Fire

Planet: Sun

Intelligence: Nakhiel

Colors: Dark red and gold

Direction: Southeast

Sorath is the most powerful of all the spirits. However, he is reserved and speaks only when absolutely necessary. He rules authority, power, leadership, and achievement. He also rules games, sports, and other forms of physical recreation. He gets along well with Bartzabel, Chasmodai, Hismael, and Kedemel, but Taphthartharath and Zazel consider him an enemy.

Kedemel

Gender: Female

Element: Water

Planet: Venus

Intelligence: Hagiel

Colors: White, green, and brown

Direction: South

Kedemel is warm, friendly, and attractive. She rules creativity, social activities, beauty, love, female sexuality, and the emotions. She gets along well with all the spirits, except for Zazel, whom she considers to be an enemy.

Taphthartharath

Gender: Hermaphrodite

Element: Water

Planet: Mercury

Intelligence: Tiriel

Colors: Pale gray, sky blue, and iridescent colors

Direction: Southwest

Taphthartharath is quick-witted, changeable, and cold. He/she rules communications, learning, intellectual pursuits, trade, economics, and healing. He/she also rules gambling, deception, knavery, and theft. Taphthartharath gets along well with Hismael, Kedemel, and Zazel, but is considered an enemy by Bartzabel, Chasmodai, and Sorath.

Chasmodai

Gender: Female

Element: Earth

Planet: Moon

Intelligence: No single intelligence

Colors: Pale yellow and silver

Direction: North

Chasmodai is gentle, caring, and restless. Sorath is the most powerful of the spirits, but Chasmodai comes a close second. Chasmodai rules change, variety, travel, the subconscious, psychic phenomena, dreams, and the unknown. She also rules biological cycles of all kinds, including reproduction. Because the Moon has no single intelligence, the angel (Gabriel) or goddess (Diana) of the Moon is usually invoked instead. Alternatively, the intelligence of intelligences (Malkah be-Tarshishim ve-ad Ruachoth Shechalim) and the spirit of spirits (Shad Barshemoth ha-Shartathan) may be invoked. Chasmodai gets along well with Hismael, Kedemel, Sorath, and Taphtharharath, but is considered an enemy by Bartzabel and Zazel.

Ritual to Invoke the Genius

The ritual begins by speaking to the Genius you have selected while drawing an Invoking Pentagram of the Earth on a sheet of paper. An invoking pentagram is one that is drawn with a line from the top point of the pentagram down to the bottom left, up two-thirds of the page to the right, across to the left, down to the right, and up again to the starting point. As geomancy is a form of earth divination, the Invoking Pentagram of the Earth plays an important role in the magic ritual performed at the start of the proceedings.

The sigil of the Genius you have chosen is then placed in the center of the pentagram. The sigil is created using numerology and magic squares. The name of the spirit is spelled out in Hebrew and is assigned a number, using numerology. Each number is located on a magic square that relates to the planet the spirit is concerned with, and a line is drawn to connect all the letters of the name (see chart 9A later in this chapter).

If you wish, you can create an elaborate invocation to call the Genius to your aid. Here is an example that could be used when invoking Kedemel. Face east and draw a large pentagram in the air while saying:

"I call on the great Archangel Raphael, regent of the element of Air. I request your presence, as I need your protection and guidance."

Turn to the south. Again draw a pentagram in the air while saying:

"I call on the great Archangel Michael, regent of the element of Fire. I request your presence, as I need your protection and guidance."

Turn to the west, and inscribe another pentagram in the air while saying:

"I call on the great Archangel Gabriel, regent of the element of Water. I request your presence, as I need your protection and guidance."

Turn to the north, and inscribe a large pentagram in the air while saying:

"I call on the great Archangel Uriel, regent of the element of Earth. I request your presence, as I need your protection and guidance."

Turn to face the east again. Say:

"In this sacred and protected circle, I invoke the spirit Kedemel. Come forth, Genius Kedemel, and work with me to ensure the success of this divination."

Alternatively, you may prefer to simply ask your chosen Genius to help you find an answer to your question.

After formulating the question and invoking the Genius, the four Mothers are created, followed by the Daughters, Nephews (rather than Nieces), Witnesses, and Judge. These are all created in the usual way, once the Mothers have been determined.

The two Witnesses and the Judge may provide all the information necessary to obtain a satisfactory answer. If more information is required, the figures are placed into the twelve houses of the horoscope in the following order:

Mother 1 is placed in the tenth house.

Mother 2 is placed in the first house.

Mother 3 is placed in the fourth house.

Mother 4 is placed in the seventh house.

Daughter 1 is placed in the eleventh house.

Daughter 2 is placed in the second house.

Daughter 3 is placed in the fifth house.

Daughter 4 is placed in the eighth house.

Nephew 1 is placed in the twelfth house.

Nephew 2 is placed in the third house.

Nephew 3 is placed in the sixth house.

Nephew 4 is placed in the ninth house.

This is slightly different to the placements used by Cornelius Agrippa. He placed the first Mother in house one, the second in house ten, the third in house seven, and the fourth in house four. Likewise, he placed the first Daughter in house two, the second in house eleven, the third in house eight, and the fourth in house five. Agrippa also had his unique way of creating the four Nieces, which went into houses three, six, nine, and twelve. Both systems ensure that the Mothers, Daughters, and Nieces appear in all four elements.

The planets and the twelve signs of the zodiac are placed in position in the usual way. The sign that relates to the figure in the first house is placed outside this house, and the other signs follow counterclockwise around the circle.

If the question involves money, the Part of Fortune is determined by adding up all the points of the first twelve figures, and dividing them by twelve. Whatever number remains indicates the house that relates to the Part of Fortune. If there is no remainder, the Part of Fortune is in the twelfth house.

The chart is examined using the methods described in chapters 5 and 6. Particular attention is paid to the house that relates to the question. However, as many of the Golden Dawn students had only recently started to learn astrology, lists were provided that gave instant answers to their questions. This rather simplistic approach to answering questions is likely to be one of the main reasons that the early students of the Golden Dawn paid scant attention to geomancy as they worked their way through the Zelator grade.

The relative strength of the figure in the house that relates to the question is noted. This is done using the planet that corresponds to the figure on the next page. This process measures the "essential dignity of the figure."

Attention was also paid to other houses that had the same figure as the one in the house that related to the question.

The aspects relating to the figure in the house in question are also examined.

The final stage of the reading is to look at the figure in the fourth house to determine the outcome of the question. If this figure fails to provide an answer, a Reconciler

House	Strongest	Very Strong	Strong	Weak	Weakest
First	Mars	Sun	Jupiter	Saturn	Venus
Second	Venus	Moon	Jupiter		Mars
Third	Mercury		Saturn		Jupiter
Fourth	Moon	Jupiter	Mercury	Mars	Saturn
Fifth	Sun		Mars		Saturn
Sixth	Mercury		Saturn	Venus	Jupiter
Seventh	Venus	Saturn	Jupiter	Sun	Mars
Eighth	Mars		Sun	Moon	Venus
Ninth	Jupiter		Venus		Mercury
Tenth	Saturn	Mars	Mercury	Jupiter	Moon
Eleventh	Saturn			Sun	
Twelfth	Jupiter	Venus			Mercury

can be created by adding together the first Mother and the Judge. However, this figure should only be created if the outcome is inconclusive.

Here are the lists of answers:

Acquisitio

Generally good for profit and gain.

First house: Positive, indicating happiness and success in all areas of life.

Second house: Highly prosperous.

Third house: Recognition and wealth.

Fourth house: Good fortune and success.

Fifth house: Success.

Sixth house: Good—especially if it agrees with the fifth.

Seventh house: Reasonably good.

Eighth house: Mildly positive. Not good for people who are unwell.

Ninth house: Good in all demands.

Tenth house: Good for legal matters.

Eleventh house: Good for all financial matters.

Twelfth house: Difficult time financially, with a strong possibility of loss.

Amissio

Good for loss of substance and sometimes for love, but very bad for gain.

First house: Negative in all areas of life.

Second house: Difficult time financially, but good for love.

Third house: Negative time. You might win an argument, but gain no satisfaction from doing so.

Fourth house: Negative for all endeavors.

Fifth house: Negative for all endeavors, except agriculture.

Sixth house: Difficult time for matters involving love and romance.

Seventh house: Good time for love, but negative for everything else.

Eighth house: Excellent for all questions.

Ninth house: Negative for all endeavors.

Tenth house: Negative for all endeavors, except for dealings with women.

Eleventh house: Good time for love, but negative for everything else.

Twelfth house: Negative for all endeavors.

Fortuna Major

Good for gain in all things where a person has hopes to win.

First house: Good for all matters, except those involving secrets.

Second house: Good for all endeavors, except dealings that involve sad thoughts or memories.

Third house: Good for all endeavors.

Fourth house: Good for all endeavors, except those involving sad thoughts.

Fifth house: Very good for all endeavors.

Sixth house: Very good for all endeavors, except those involving lust and debauchery.

Seventh house: Good for all endeavors.

Eighth house: Reasonably good for all endeavors.

Ninth house: Very good for all endeavors.

Tenth house: Extremely good for all endeavors. Ask for what you want at this time.

Eleventh house: Very good for all endeavors.

Twelfth house: Good for all endeavors.

Fortuna Minor

Good in any manner in which a person wishes to proceed quickly.

First house: Good for all matters involving competition and love.

Second house: Very good for all endeavors.

Third house: Good for all endeavors, as long as you remain calm.

Fourth house: Negative for all endeavors, except those involving peace and harmony.

Fifth house: Good for all endeavors.

Sixth house: Moderately good for all endeavors.

Seventh house: Negative for all matters, except love and competition.

Eighth house: Negative for all endeavors.

Ninth house: Good for all endeavors, as long as you keep your temper in check.

Tenth house: Good for all matters, except those involving peace and quiet.

Eleventh house: Good for all endeavors, especially love.

Twelfth house: Good for all endeavors that you perform for yourself.

Laetitia

Good for joy, present or to come.

First house: Good for all endeavors, as long as you avoid strife and disagreements.

Second house: Good for resting and thinking.

Third house: Pay attention to your health.

Fourth house: Positive for all endeavors.

Fifth house: Extremely good for all endeavors.

Sixth house: Negative for all endeavors.

Seventh house: Neither good nor bad for all endeavors.

Eighth house: Negative for all endeavors.

Ninth house: Very good for all endeavors.

Tenth house: Good for any matters involving competition.

Eleventh house: Good for all endeavors.

Twelfth house: Negative for all endeavors.

Tristitia

Evil in almost all things.

First house: Moderately good for all endeavors, especially matters concerning investments.

Second house: Mildly positive for all matters.

Third house: Negative for all endeavors.

Fourth house: Negative for all endeavors.

Fifth house: Negative for all endeavors. Take your time, and think and analyze before moving forward.

Sixth house: Negative for all matters, except those involving lust and debauchery.

Seventh house: Negative for anything involving money or inheritances.

Eighth house: Negative for all concerns, except for those involving secrets.

Ninth house: Negative for all endeavors.

Tenth house: Negative for all endeavors, except those involving strengthening personal finances.

Eleventh house: Negative for all endeavors.

Twelfth house: Negative for all endeavors.

Puella

Good in all demands, especially with regard to women.

First house: Good for all endeavors, except for arguments and disagreements.

Second house: Very good for all endeavors.

Third house: Good for all endeavors.

Fourth house: Neither good nor bad.

Fifth house: Very good for all endeavors. However, check the aspects.

Sixth house: Good for all endeavors, especially those involving sexual activity.

Seventh house: Good for all matters, except for arguments and disagreements.

Eighth house: Good for all endeavors.

Ninth house: Reasonably good for all concerns, but especially good for matters involving music.

Tenth house: Good for anything involving peace and harmony.

Eleventh house: Good for all matters, especially those involving women.

Twelfth house: Good for all endeavors.

Puer

Evil in most demands, except in those things relating to war or love.

First house: Neither good nor bad.

Second house: Good for all endeavors, but expect difficulties from time to time.

Third house: Good for all endeavors, especially those involving money and investments.

Fourth house: Negative in all matters, except those involving competition and love.

Fifth house: Moderately good for all concerns.

Sixth house: Moderately good for all endeavors.

Seventh house: Negative for all endeavors, except those involving strife.

Eighth house: Negative for all endeavors, except those involving love.

Ninth house: Negative for all endeavors, except those involving competition.

Tenth house: Slightly negative, but good for matters involving love and romance.

Eleventh house: Moderately good for all endeavors.

Twelfth house: Very good for all endeavors.

Rubeus

Evil in all that is good, and good in all that is evil.

First house: Destroy the figure if Rubeus is in the first house. The judgment is worthless if Rubeus is in this position.

Second house: Negative for all endeavors.

Third house: Negative for all endeavors.

Fourth house: Negative for all endeavors, except those involving competition.

Fifth house: Negative for all matters, except for love and romance.

Sixth house: Negative for all endeavors.

Seventh house: Negative for all endeavors, except those involving competition.

Eighth house: Negative for all endeavors.

Ninth house: Extremely negative for all endeavors. Wait patiently for as long as necessary.

Tenth house: Extremely negative for all endeavors.

Eleventh house: Negative for all endeavors.

Twelfth house: Negative for all endeavors.

Albus

Good for profit and for entering into a place or undertaking.

First house: Good for anything involving peace, love, and marriage.

Second house: Good for all endeavors.

Third house: Very good for all endeavors.

Fourth house: Very good for all endeavors, except those involving disagreements with others.

Fifth house: Good for all endeavors.

Sixth house: Good for all endeavors.

Seventh house: Good for all endeavors, except those involving conflicts and disagreements.

Eighth house: Good for all endeavors.

Ninth house: Good news is about to appear.

Tenth house: Extremely good for all endeavors.

Eleventh house: Very good for all endeavors.

Twelfth house: Extremely positive for all endeavors.

Conjunctio

Good with good, or evil with evil. Recovery of things lost.

First house: Positive for all matters involving good, but negative for anything involving bad.

Second house: Moderately good for all endeavors.

Third house: Good fortune.

Fourth house: Good for all endeavors, except health. Check the figure in the eighth house for more information.

Fifth house: Moderately good for all endeavors.

Sixth house: Neither good nor bad.

Seventh house: Good for all endeavors.

Eighth house: Negative for all endeavors.

Ninth house: Moderately good for all endeavors.

Tenth house: Good for matters involving love, but negative for matters involving health concerns.

Eleventh house: Good for all endeavors.

Twelfth house: Moderately good for all endeavors.

Carcer

Generally evil. Delay, binding, bar, restriction.

First house: Negative for all endeavors, except for those involving personal security.

Second house: Negative for all endeavors.

Third house: Extremely negative for all endeavors.

Fourth house: Negative for all endeavors.

Fifth house: You should receive news in the next few days. Negative for all endeavors.

Sixth house: Extremely negative for all endeavors.

Seventh house: Negative for all endeavors.

Eighth house: Extremely negative for all endeavors.

Ninth house: Negative for all endeavors.

Tenth house: Negative for all endeavors.

Eleventh house: A stressful time.

Twelfth house: Good for all endeavors.

Caput Draconis

Good with good, evil with evil. Give a good issue for gain.

First house: Good for all endeavors.

Second house: Good for all endeavors.

Third house: Very good for all endeavors.

Fourth house: Good for all endeavors, except for those involving disagreements with others.

Fifth house: Very good for all endeavors.

Sixth house: Neither good nor bad.

Seventh house: Good for all endeavors, especially those involving peace and harmony.

Eighth house: Good for all endeavors.

Ninth house: Very good for all endeavors.

Tenth house: Good for all endeavors.

Eleventh house: Good for anything involving spiritual growth.

Twelfth house: Slightly negative for all endeavors.

Cauda Draconis

Good with evil, and evil with good. Good for loss, and for passing.

First house: Destroy the chart if Cauda Draconis appears here. Cauda Draconis in this position makes the judgment worthless.

Second house: Extremely negative for all endeavors.

Third house: Negative for all endeavors.

Fourth house: Positive for all endeavors, especially those that are coming to an end.

Fifth house: Extremely negative for all endeavors.

Sixth house: Moderately good for all endeavors.

Seventh house: Negative for all endeavors.

Eighth house: Neither good nor bad. Be patient.

Ninth house: Positive for anything involving science or technology. Negative for anything involving travel.

Tenth house: Negative for all endeavors.

Eleventh house: Negative for all endeavors, except helping others.

Twelfth house: Good for all endeavors.

Via

Injurious to the goodness of other figures generally, but good for journeys and voyages.

First house: Negative for all endeavors.

Second house: Neither good nor bad.

Third house: Very good for all endeavors.

Fourth house: Good for all endeavors, except those involving love and romance.

Fifth house: Good for travel.

Sixth house: Negative for all endeavors.

Seventh house: Moderately good, especially for travel.

Eighth house: Negative for all endeavors.

Ninth house: Neither good nor bad. However, good for journeys.

Tenth house: Good for all endeavors.

Eleventh house: Very good for all endeavors.

Twelfth house: Extremely good for all endeavors.

Populus

Sometimes good and sometimes bad; good with good, and evil with evil.

First house: Good for anything involving love, romance, and marriage.

Second house: Moderately good for all endeavors.

Third house: Slightly positive for all endeavors.

Fourth house: Good for all endeavors, except for love.

Fifth house: Good for all endeavors.

Sixth house: Good for all endeavors.

Seventh house: Slightly positive for all endeavors.

Eighth house: Negative for all endeavors.

Ninth house: You may need to search for the information you need in order to progress.

Tenth house: Good for all endeavors.

Eleventh house: Good for all endeavors.

Twelfth house: Extremely negative for all endeavors.

Example

For the sake of example, let's say you've asked, "Will I sell my home for a good price?"

You create the chart in the normal manner. The four Mothers are Acquisitio, Puer, Laetitia, and Tristitia:

First Mother	Second Mother	Third Mother	Fourth Mother
O O	O	O	O O
O	O	O O	O O
O O	O O	O O	O O
O	O	O O	O
Acquisitio	Puer	Laetitia	Tristitia

The four Daughters are Conjunctio, Fortuna Minor, Populus, and Puer:

First Daughter	Second Daughter	Third Daughter	Fourth Daughter
O O	O	O O	O
O	O	O O	O
O	O O	O O	O O
O O	O O	O O	O
Conjunctio	Fortuna Minor	Populus	Puer

The four Nephews are Laetitia, Carcer, Amissio, and Puer:

First Nephew	Second Nephew	Third Nephew	Fourth Nephew
O	O	O	O
O O	O O	O O	O
O O	O O	O	O O
O O	O	O O	O
Laetitia	Carcer	Amissio	Puer

The two Witnesses are Caput Draconis and Tristitia:

Left Witness	Right Witness
O O	O O
O	O O
O	O O
O	O
Caput Draconis	Tristitia

The Judge is Conjunctio:

Judge
O O
O
O
O O
Conjunctio

The figures are placed in their respective houses (see chart 9A).

Real estate is a fourth house matter. As the question involves money, you need to find out where the Part of Fortune is. This is done by adding up all the dots that compose the Mothers, Daughters, and Nephews, and dividing the total by 12. The total is 74. The number 74 divided by 12 is 6, with a remainder of 2. This places the Part of Fortune in the second house.

You can now check the meanings of the figures in the houses using the list above.

Laetitia in the fourth house is "positive for all endeavors."

Laetitia relates to Jupiter, which is very strong in this house.

Laetitia is also in the twelfth house. Jupiter is at its strongest in this position.

Fortuna Minor in the second house is "very good for all endeavors." Fortuna Minor relates to the Sun, which has little effect in this position.

Puer in the first house is "neither good nor bad." Puer relates to Mars, which is at its strongest in this position. Puer is also in the eighth and ninth houses. These are negative signs, but have no bearing on this particular reading.

Cancer in the fourth house favors home and family, including the physical property.

There are no aspects that relate to the question.

The two Witnesses and the Judge are not particularly helpful, as they indicate an indifferent result.

However, Laetitia in the fourth house shows that the final outcome will prove satisfactory. Consequently, you will receive a reasonably good price for your home when you sell it.

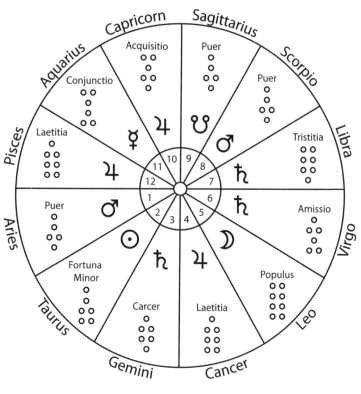

Chart 9A

Aleister Crowley

Aleister Crowley (1875–1947), the controversial English occultist and writer, was initiated into the Hermetic Order of the Golden Dawn in 1898. However, senior members of the order in London, believing he was a homosexual, accused him of "moral turpitude" and refused to let him advance to the Adeptus Minor grade. Crowley had successfully completed the course of work set for members of the Outer Order, and was entitled to progress. Crowley went to Paris to see Samuel Liddell Mathers, the head of the order, who initiated him into the Adeptus Minor grade on January 16, 1900. The frustration and anger that this caused was the final straw for the adepts in London, who tried to expel Mathers from the order. These actions became part of a series of events that ultimately led to the downfall of the order.

Crowley was a talented author and poet. His book on geomancy, *A Handbook of Geomancy*, was first published in *The Equinox* (vol. I, no. 2), an occult magazine that Crowley established in 1909. The method he used was similar to that taught by the Golden Dawn. However, he used the sigil of the ruling planet that related to the question being asked. This sigil was drawn in the middle of the pentagram while thinking of the question. The pen should not be removed from the paper until the sigil is complete. Surprisingly, Crowley made no mention of the ruling spirit, or Genius.

In his system there are seven possible sigils:

Saturn (♄): For questions relating to agriculture, sorrow, and death.

Jupiter (♃): For questions relating to good fortune, feasting, and church preferment.

Mars ($\male$): For questions relating to war, victory, and fighting.

Sun ($\odot$): For questions relating to power and magistracy.

Venus ($\female$): For questions relating to love, music, and pleasure.

Mercury ($\mercury$): For questions relating to science, learning, and knavery.

Moon ($\leftmoon$): For questions relating to travel and outdoor pursuits.

In the next chapter we'll look at a completely different form of geomancy known as Arthurian divination.

ten

Arthurian Divination

When I was twenty-one, I spent several months living in Cornwall, in England. As I mentioned in the introduction to this book, it was an exciting time for me, because for the first time I met other people who were as interested in the psychic world as I was. I was invited to join several groups, made many friends, and learned a great deal.

I was introduced to Arthurian divination during this time. This system uses numerology, which I was familiar with, and geomancy, which was totally new to me at the time. A friend helped me make my first set of rune sticks so I could create the nine geomantic figures that were used in this form of divination. While working on these, he talked endlessly about King Arthur; Uther Pendragon, who was Arthur's father; and Merlin, who advised both of them.

He also told me about the *Vita Merlini*, a biography of Merlin that was written by Geoffrey of Monmouth in about 1150.[1] Along with the story of Merlin, the *Vita Merlini* contained a great deal of Celtic lore, cosmology, natural history, classical mythology, and elemental psychology. It also included the Wheel of Life (see the chart on the next page). All of these things had been part of an oral tradition for many centuries, but Geoffrey of Monmouth was one of the first to write them down.

Although it's called the Wheel of Life, it is actually a spiral, and Merlin went around the Wheel many times in the course of the *Vita Merlini*, growing spiritually and undergoing nine transformations of consciousness. These are:

Grief or guilt (north)

Compassion (northeast)

Disorientation (east)

Sexual liberation (southeast)

Foresight (south)

Cosmic vision (southwest)

Curative transformation (west)

Liberation from temptation (northwest)

Spiritual enlightenment (north)

While doing all of this, Merlin also experienced hardship in winter, recalled love in spring, participated in a

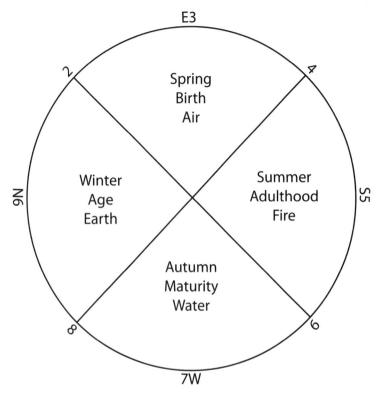

The Wheel of Life

contest of will in summer, and learned how to benefit from experience in autumn.

Consequently, the Wheel can be interpreted on a number of levels, all of which emphasize growth, development, and ultimate wisdom. Arthurian divination is a modern form of numerological geomancy using the Wheel of Life. The nine single digits of numerology cover most facets of human experience. Combined with the geomantic figures, they provide a clear picture of the situation and its conclusion. In addition, they show how the outcome will affect other areas of a person's life.

Here are the basic meanings for the nine digits:

Number One

One relates to the individual. It represents independence and attainment. A good figure in this position indicates a successful outcome. However, a negative figure in this position indicates difficulties that have to be overcome. These difficulties usually relate to the person asking the question and can relate to pride, arrogance, stubbornness, ego, and a rigid approach to life.

Number Two

In numerology, two is the number of tact, diplomacy, and close relationships. A good figure in this position is an indication that the relationship will grow and develop. It also shows that the person is adaptable, able to get along well with others, and willing to compromise when necessary. This person will also be considerate of other people's feelings. It is a sign of happiness, success, and contentment. A negative figure in this position shows that the person creates problems by failing to look after the needs of others, especially his or her partner.

Number Three

Three is the number of self-expression, communication, and experiencing the joys of life. A positive figure in this position shows that the person is happy, well-adjusted, and capable of expressing himself or herself effectively. This person will also be affectionate, enthusiastic, and optimistic. There might be a tendency for this person to spend too much time on frivolous activities. A negative figure in this position indicates that the person has a gloomy, pessimistic approach to life, and is likely to make mistakes in expressing himself or herself.

Number Four

Four is the number of hard work, and system and order. A good figure in this position shows that the person is prepared to work long and hard to achieve his or her goals. This person will be well-organized and will perform all the necessary tasks in a logical progression. This person will also be reliable, dependable, and willing to give a hand when necessary. A negative figure in this position shows that the person lacks motivation and feels restricted, limited, and hemmed in by circumstances. This person is likely to take shortcuts that potentially jeopardize the success of whatever it is he or she is working on.

Number Five

Five is the number of freedom, variety, and change. It also represents adventure, expansion, enthusiasm, and boundless optimism. A positive figure in this position shows that the person will receive many opportunities and has the potential to capitalize on them. This is an entrepreneurial number that bodes well for business. A negative figure in this position shows that the person is wasting his or her abilities and letting opportunities pass by. This person may become lost in overindulgence and blame everyone else for a lack of success.

Number Six

Six represents the domestic side of life, and is the number of home and family responsibilities. A positive figure in this position shows the person will experience love and support from his or her loved ones, and will also be caring, loving, and supportive in return. Six indicates that love sent out will return multiplied. A negative figure here is a sign that the person is unhappy with home and family life, and may feel resentful when helping others. He or she is likely to feel guilty about these feelings. Sometimes, this person may become overwhelmed with everyone else's problems and be taken advantage of by others.

Number Seven

Seven is the number of wisdom, analysis, and understanding. It relates to spirituality, intuition, study, and contemplation. A positive figure in this position shows the person will be prepared to listen to his or her inner self, and will need time for quiet meditation and contemplation. A negative figure in this position shows the person ignores the spiritual side of life and works entirely on the material plane.

Number Eight

Eight is the number of money and material satisfaction. A positive figure in this position shows the person will be ambitious and will work long and hard until he or she receives the desired financial reward from the activity. This person is realistic, practical, and down-to-earth in his or her approach. He or she is willing to work hard and is persistent and clearly focused on the end result. A negative figure in this position shows that the person will seek money and financial success in such a way that all other areas of life are forgotten or ignored. Consequently, the money, once achieved, will provide little in the way of pleasure or satisfaction.

Number Nine

Nine is the number of humanitarianism, compassion, and understanding. Six and nine are both caring numbers. Six gives to loved ones. Nine is more universal and gives to humanity in general. A positive figure in this position shows that the person is compassionate, understanding, and caring in his or her dealings with others. This person will give, even when there is no possibility of any return. A negative figure in this position shows that the person focuses entirely on his or her needs, and ignores the needs and feelings of anyone else.

Groupings of Figures and Numbers

There are also two main groups of figures. One, four, and eight are all good numbers for business. If the figures in these positions are all favorable, the outlook is extremely positive from a business point of view.

Three, six, and nine are all creative numbers. Good figures in these positions are a good sign for any form of creativity or self-expression. These are also good numbers for helping others. Six and nine are both humanitarian numbers, and three is the number of self-expression. Good communication skills enable you to help others effectively.

Specific and General Questions

It is preferable to ask specific questions, but Arthurian divination also enables you to obtain a good general reading by asking a general question, such as "What will next year be like?" or "What does the future hold?" or "Will I be happy in the future?"

The figures are created after the question has been asked. Initially, I used my rune sticks to create the nine figures. However, any method that feels right for you will work well. The first figure to be generated goes into position one on the Wheel of Life. The second figure goes into position two, and so on. Each figure is generated individually, and is not derived by combining other figures. The same figure can be generated a number of times. In fact, on one memorable occasion, I cast the same figure seven times in a row. Interestingly enough, this provided the perfect answer to the question.

Let's assume your question is "Will Jason and Kylie get married this year?" You generate the nine figures and place them in their respective positions around the Wheel of Life. Let's say you generated the following figures:

1. Puer
2. Laetitia
3. Conjunctio
4. Via
5. Rubeus
6. Caput Draconis
7. Amissio
8. Fortuna Major
9. Conjunctio

Because the question relates to marriage, you start by looking at the figure beside number two. Two is the number of close relationships, and a good figure here indicates a relationship that grows and develops. In this instance, Laetitia is in this position. Laetitia is a positive figure that indicates a forward movement that is favorable for the person asking the question.

When someone marries, he or she takes on home and—possibly—family responsibilities. This relates to number six. Caput Draconis in this position represents new starts. As Caput Draconis is favorable in any question that involves beginnings, it is highly positive in this position.

You could stop at this point, if you wished, as the question has been answered. However, you can also look at the figures in the other positions and see how they relate to the question.

Number one is Puer. One represents independence. Puer is energetic, enthusiastic, and desires change. It is also immature and frequently acts without thinking. This could create problems; when someone gets married, he or she has to give up a degree of independence.

Number three is Conjunctio. Three relates to self-expression. Conjunctio indicates the union of opposites, which could relate to marriage. The combination of three and Conjunctio shows there'll be plenty of conversation in this marriage.

Number four is Via. Four relates to hard work, and system and order. Via indicates change and is positive for all journeys. Marriage is most certainly a journey. This combination shows that hard work will be required from time to time to ensure the success of the marriage.

Number five is Rubeus. Five relates to adventure, freedom, change, and variety. Rubeus is usually a negative figure, but is positive in matters relating to sexuality. Jason and Kylie are likely to enjoy an uninhibited, active sex life together.

Number seven is Amissio. Seven relates to wisdom and understanding. Amissio indicates a loss. This is usually negative, but can be positive if a loss is desired. In this case, Kylie and Jason could be losing their hearts, and gaining wisdom and understanding as a result.

Number eight is Fortuna Major. Eight relates to money, finances, and large-scale undertakings. Fortuna Major in this position is extremely positive and is an indication that the married couple will enjoy worldly success as well.

Number nine is Conjunctio. Nine is the compassionate, caring, humanitarian number. Conjunctio in this position shows that Jason and Kylie will work together in a harmonious and compassionate manner.

Using Arthurian divination, we not only answered the question, but were also able to provide a great deal of additional information as well. This is one of the major benefits of this form of reading.

Spiritual Growth

You will have noticed that in this particular reading we did not use any of the information in the center of the circle (spring, birth, Air, and so on). This information is used for questions relating to spiritual growth and development. The Wheel of Life is extremely useful for this type of question, as you can follow the person's development from the earliest stages (winter, Earth) through spring, summer, autumn, and ultimately back to winter again.

Here is an example. Your question might be: "Am I following the right spiritual path for me?" You create nine figures:

1. Via

2. Albus

3. Laetitia

4. Fortuna Minor

5. Carcer

6. Via

7. Puella

8. Albus

9. Caput Draconis

You began your spiritual quest in the right way. Number one represents new starts, and you have Via in this position, indicating forward movement and progress. It will not be quick progress, as you are in Earth, but all the same, this indicates a good start.

Number two is still in Earth, which represents patient waiting. Albus is a good figure to have in this position, as it indicates quiet, gentle progress. It also relates well to beginnings, which is where you are at this point.

With number three you move into Air and spring. Air is enthusiastic, communicative, and full of the joys of life. Spring indicates new life. In this position is Laetitia, a highly enthusiastic figure that indicates forward progress and success. This is a strong indication of significant progress at this time.

Number four is still in spring, but it's slightly less naïve and more rigid in outlook. You have Fortuna Minor in this position. This indicates fast progress, but is also a warning that the success you gain now may only be temporary.

With number five you move into summer. This period is also represented by adulthood and Fire. You still have plenty of enthusiasm and energy, but you're no longer as naïve as you were. Carcer in this position indicates delays and restrictions. However, as your spiritual growth requires time on your own, this enforced isolation might help you progress inwardly.

With number six you are still in summer. Because of this number, your thoughts are likely to be focused on home and family matters. Via indicates change, and in this position it may well indicate a change in outlook, especially when it comes to family concerns.

With number seven you move into autumn and maturity. You are looking at life differently now, as you have grown and matured as a result of everything that occurred during winter, spring, and summer. Since seven is a spiritual number, this should be an excellent time for spiritual growth. Puella is usually a favorable figure, but it is more concerned with temporary, rather than permanent, progress. This will prove to be a happy time, but you may not achieve all the success you desired during this period.

Number eight is also in autumn. Its main focus is finances and material success. Albus represents peace and growth of wisdom. You will certainly develop spiritually at this point. Interestingly, even though it won't be your major concern, your finances should also improve, as Albus favors business matters.

The circle is completed when you move into number nine. You are back into winter again, and progress will be slow but steady. In this position you have Caput Draconis, which indicates new beginnings, with exciting possibilities. This is a favorable figure to have in this position, as it will give you the necessary enthusiasm to continue moving forward throughout the bleakest time of year.

Your quest is not necessarily over. The Wheel of Life is a spiral, and you can move around it as many times as are necessary to learn the lessons and to achieve your goal.

The Nine Transformations of Consciousness

You can also read the Wheel of Life using the nine transformations of consciousness in the *Vita Merlini*. You do not need to ask a question when using the transformations, as they are used only for determining spiritual growth.

Let's assume you cast the following figures:

1. Conjunctio

2. Amissio

3. Puer

4. Laetitia

5. Laetitia

6. Populus

7. Acquisitio

8. Populus

9. Laetitia

This shows that you start your path with Conjunctio and the transformation of grief or guilt. This would indicate that someone else helps you handle and deal with this transformation.

The second transformation is where you learn compassion. Amissio in this position shows that you learn compassion through a loss of some sort. As Amissio indicates something that is just out of reach, compassion might be a hard lesson to learn. However, Amissio is traditionally considered a generous figure, and this can play a part in a compassionate approach to life.

The third transformation is disorientation. This means that, although you've made progress in the previous two transformations, you will be feeling uncertain about where to go from here. You're likely to be experiencing conflicting emotions and may be feeling nervous and insecure. Puer in this position is a positive figure. Puer represents transformation and change. It is passionate, forceful, and courageous. Although it can be argumentative and thoughtless, the enthusiasm and energy of Puer ensures success.

The fourth transformation is sexual liberation. This can be a difficult transformation for many people, but Laetitia in this position provides joy, happiness, and forward progress. Laetitia relates to the expansive planet Jupiter and the emotional water sign of Pisces, both of whom are ideal for this particular transformation.

The fifth transformation is foresight. At this stage, you are using logic, while also learning to accept and trust your intuition. Laetitia appears in both the fourth and fifth transformations. In this position, Laetitia is able to express joy, delight, and happiness. You will receive enormous pleasure and satisfaction as you learn this transformation.

The sixth transformation is cosmic vision. This is where your awareness expands and you gain knowledge and understanding of the hidden truths. You have Populus in this position, showing that other people will be involved in helping you learn this transformation.

In the seventh transformation, you learn curative transformation. At this stage you learn how to heal yourself and others with the healing power of love. Acquisitio in this position shows that you will not only be successful, but also that the prize will be well within reach.

The eighth transformation is liberation from temptation. At this stage you learn how to deal with the various temptations, especially the pleasures of the flesh that most people find hard to overcome. The figure here is Populus.

This shows that other people will be involved in aiding—and abetting—you as you learn this difficult transformation.

Finally, you reach the ninth transformation of spiritual enlightenment. You are likely to have thought you had reached this stage on many occasions while working on this quest. It is only once you reach this transformation that you'll realize how much more work and effort are required to reach ultimate perfection and become one with God. Laetitia appears for the third time in your chart. Laetitia is an extremely positive figure that is willing to help you achieve this final goal. Laetitia indicates upward movement, and is an excellent indicator of success. Once you learn to forget yourself and truly become one with God, the goal is reached.

It is possible to reach perfection in just one circuit of the Wheel of Life. However, it is more usual for a person to make several revolutions around the Wheel, learning a little bit more each time. These circuits may well be spread over several lifetimes. It is also possible for a person to become stuck at a particular transformation, and find it impossible to progress further in this lifetime.

Back in the early 1990s, I conducted a series of workshops on Arthurian divination. A young man with poor social skills attended one of these. I'll call him Carl, as I cannot remember his name. Carl was incredibly shy and sat in the back row, as far away from the other attendees as possible. I tried to include him in the workshop, but he refused to participate. The other students also tried to engage him in conversation, but without success. He obviously preferred to be on his own.

Consequently, I was surprised when Carl came up to me at the end of the second day and asked if we could have a private chat. Once everyone else had left, we sat down and I asked him how he was enjoying the workshop.

"It's good. Thank you," he replied.

There was a long silence until I asked him how I could help him. He opened up his bag and brought out the chart he had constructed for the nine transformations of consciousness.

"This isn't good, is it?" he asked.

At first glance, it seemed to be the most difficult chart of this sort that I'd seen. He had cast:

1. Puer

2. Carcer

3. Carcer

4. Carcer

5. Carcer

6. Tristitia

7. Rubeus

8. Via

9. Caput Draconis

I studied the chart for a minute or two before answering.

"Let's see what this tells us," I said. "You start your path with Puer and the transformation of grief or guilt. With Puer in this position, you were probably rash, impulsive, and most likely rather naïve. You were probably experiencing a sense of grief or guilt because of something you did, or at least thought you did. You would have gradually reached maturity during this transformation.

"There's nothing out of the way, or unusual, about this transformation. However, it's followed by Carcer for the next four transformations. That's certainly unusual, and you must have gone through an extremely difficult time as you made your way through them.

"As you know, the second transformation relates to compassion and clarity of thought. You were probably timid and afraid. You might have felt isolated, for some reason. Consequently, you built a shell around yourself that no one could penetrate. Even if you felt compassion, you were unable to express it, as you were confined in your own private prison.

"The third transformation is disorientation. It's a stage of insecurity. You were probably uncertain as to where to go from here. Of course, with Carcer here again, you contained all that insecurity and pain inside you. Other people probably found you rigid, stubborn, and hard to get along with. They probably failed to see the pain you were suffering inside.

"The fourth transformation relates to sexual liberation. This is a difficult time for many people, but it was made even harder for you as you were still locked inside your self-imposed prison. One of the keywords for Carcer is *delay*, so you probably delayed, or denied, this particular transformation. This would have increased your sense of isolation.

"The fifth transformation is foresight. This is thinking, making plans, and learning to trust your intuition. With Carcer in this position, you wallowed in your feelings of isolation, and would have experienced many more negative thoughts than positive ones. Your feelings of detachment and the huge amounts of time you spent on your own may have helped your intuition, just as long as the negativity was kept under control.

"The sixth transformation is cosmic vision. This is a stage where you expand your awareness and gain knowledge of the hidden truths. You're finally free of Carcer, which was, in effect, a prison, but now you have Tristitia, which relates to sorrow. Because of what you've been through in the other transformations, Tristitia suggests more pain. However, although it relates to loss of confidence and lowered expectations, Tristitia also gives you the opportunity to look at your life in a completely new way. The lesson of this vision might take time and be difficult, even painful, at times, but you will learn a great deal during this transformation.

"The seventh transformation is curative transformation. At this stage you're learning to heal yourself and others with the healing power of love. Rubeus is a challenging figure, and as it's self-centered and concerned primarily with its own gratification, you may feel that it makes it impossible to learn this transformation. In fact, it encourages you to become more passionately involved in life, and this can help you relate better with others, and also yourself. However, it's not an easy lesson to learn, and you probably struggled during this transformation.

"The eighth transformation is liberation from temptation. Most people are easily tempted by the pleasures of the flesh, and have to reach this stage before they can start to overcome these temptations. Because of the negative figures in the previous transformations, you may feel that you've overcome these temptations. However, in reality, in your mind you will have wallowed in them as much, if not more, than most people. Via is an indication of change. During this transformation your attitude to life will change enormously, and you'll feel more positive about the future than ever before.

"The ninth transformation is spiritual enlightenment. You may feel that you've already reached this point, but once inside this transformation, you, like everyone else, will realize just how much work and effort is required to achieve ultimate perfection. Caput Draconis is an excellent figure to have here because it is a sign of new beginnings, with a positive outcome. It shows that every aspect of your life is improving."

Carl nodded. "I understand that," he said. "My concern is . . ." To my surprise, he suddenly burst into tears, and I hugged and consoled him for a while before he was able to continue.

"I've had a terrible life so far," he told me. "My parents separated just after I was born, and my mother became an alcoholic. She drank sherry all day long, and that seemed to make her even more depressed. I was never close to her, and I couldn't cry when she died. I think she blamed me for the breakup of her marriage. After she died, I went into foster care, and I was sexually abused by both of my foster parents. Eventually, I ended up in a home, and all the other kids teased me because I still wet the bed."

Carl continued telling me his life story, and I let him take as long as he wished, as he desperately needed to talk to someone. When he finished, he started to apologize for taking up my time.

"Thanks for sharing it with me," I told him. "I'm glad you did, as you're looking a bit brighter now. Am I the first person you've spoken to about this?"

He nodded. "I find it hard to talk about my problems." He traced the cycle on the chart. "But I'm glad I confided in you. I can understand the negative figures on my chart. But you said we have to go around this circle many, many times until we learn the lessons. Does that mean I have to experience these figures again and again?"

I shook my head and patted Carl on his shoulder. "It seems to me that you've already learned some of these lessons. What you need to do now is remain aware of them, and work hard to learn the lesson each transformation offers. You can remain in your prison for the rest of your life, if you want to. Of course, if you do that, you won't learn the lessons. It's going to take time and effort, but I think you've taken your first big step forward by confiding in me today. Take it slowly and gently. Treat others the way you would like to be treated. Confide a bit more in others. Reach out to others. It's hard to open yourself up and be vulnerable. You can—and will—be hurt at times, but the joy you'll receive will far outweigh any of the disappointments you'll get."

I stopped, as he seemed about to say something. "Thank you," he said. "Thank you very much."

The next day was the final day of the workshop. Carl came in and sat down in his usual place. I noticed that although he didn't speak, Carl nodded at people as they came into the room. When we stopped for morning coffee, Carl exchanged a few words with some of the others. I could see people exchanging glances, but no one commented out loud.

In the afternoon, I asked the attendees what they had got out of the workshop. To my surprise, Carl put up his hand. When I called on him, he came up to the front of the class, and told them about his life and how it related to the nine transformations of consciousness. He obviously found it extremely difficult, but he managed to get across everything he wanted to say. When he finished, everyone in the class applauded. Carl returned to his seat with crimson cheeks and a broad grin. Afterwards, everyone wanted to talk with him. I haven't seen him since, but I like to think that what he learned about Arthurian geomancy helped him look at his life in a different way. Hopefully, it would also help him progress in this incarnation.

In the next chapter, we'll learn how to create charts for specific days, weeks, months, or years.

eleven

Horary Geomancy

The word *horary* means "pertaining to the hour." Consequently, horary geomancy refers to a chart that is constructed for a specific length of time, such as an hour, day, week, month, year, or even longer. Horary geomancy is a useful way to find out how a particular period of time will turn out. Charts can be erected to cover any period of time and any specific purpose.

An acquaintance of mine erects horary charts to determine the best time to visit his dentist, doctor, and bank manager. He also uses it to determine the best times for important business meetings. A close friend of mine erects charts to determine the best times for her to study parapsychology.

The chart is constructed in the usual way, using whatever system appeals to you. I use the method described in chapters 5 and 6. However, my friend who is studying parapsychology prefers the method devised by Cornelius Agrippa. Once the chart has been constructed, instead of examining the first house, the house the question relates to, and the fourth house, every house is interpreted. The figure in each house provides information on how that aspect of the person's life will fare during the designated period of time.

Let's assume you want to know how next Wednesday will be for you. You create a chart (see chart 11A).

Rubeus in the first and fifth houses shows that the day does not get off to a good start, and there could be disagreements and other problems, probably involving children.

Puer in the second house shows the possibility of a sudden change in your finances. You will be enthusiastic, energetic, and may find it hard to think before acting. Do not rush into anything involving money.

Conjunctio in the third and twelfth houses indicates a meeting with your siblings, along with the possibility of discovering something that has been concealed or kept secret.

Fortuna Major in the fourth and seventh houses shows positive developments with your home and your partner.

Cauda Draconis in the sixth house shows that some matter is nearing completion, and your dealings with a tradesperson are coming to an end.

Acquisitio in the eighth and tenth houses shows it will be a successful day as far as your career is concerned. Your feelings will be strong and positive.

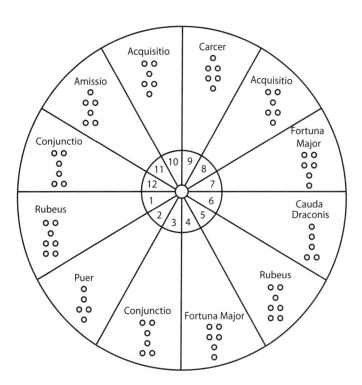

Chart 11A

Carcer in the ninth house shows it is not a good day to embark on a lengthy trip. You are unlikely to pay any attention to philosophy or spirituality at this time either.

Amissio in the eleventh house shows the likelihood of a loss involving friends, associates, or your own hopes and dreams.

The two Witnesses are Fortuna Minor, and the Judge is Populus. This shows that any success you achieve today will be with the help of others. This may well be a temporary, rather than a permanent, success. You will make more progress today if you pause and rest along the way, rather than try to force your ideas and plans onto others.

During the Middle Ages and the Renaissance, it was common for geomancers to construct lifelong charts for newborn babies to see what positive and negative influences they would experience over a lifetime. This enabled the parents to develop the child's strengths, and to turn potential weaknesses and areas of difficulty into learning experiences that would help the child later on.

Adults would also obtain Life Reading charts from time to time, to ensure that they were on track and were following their true destiny.

Horary charts can also be an extremely useful way to practice while you're learning geomancy. If you erect a chart for yourself every day for a month or two, you'll familiarize yourself with the process and at the same time will gain insights into the day ahead.

In the next chapter we'll look at something that is not true geomancy, but is related to it: Napoleon's *Book of Fate*.

twelve

Napoleon's *Book of Fate*

*T*he *Book of Fate* is by far the best known of the simplified variations of geomancy that became popular in the nineteenth century. Part of its success is due to the rather dubious association this book has with Napoleon. The title page of an early edition of this book says: *The Book of Fate, formerly in the possession of Napoleon, late Emperor of France; and now first rendered into English from a German Translation, of an Ancient Egyptian Manuscript, found in the year 1801, by M. Sonnini, in one of the Royal Tombs, near Mount Libycus, in Upper Egypt. By H. Kirchenhoffer, Fellow of the University of Pavia, &c. &c. &c.*

Herman Kirchenhoffer dedicated the book to Napoleon's widow, Her Imperial Highness Marie Louise.

M. Sonnini, who supposedly discovered the manuscript, was head of the "Commission of Arts" that accompanied Napoleon's expedition to Egypt. In 1801 he apparently discovered a sarcophagus in the interior chamber of one of the royal tombs in Mount Libycus. Attached to the left breast of a mummy he found inside the sarcophagus was a long roll of papyrus containing "hieroglyphics which were beautifully painted on it."[1] The manuscript was allegedly translated by a "learned Copt," who dictated the text to Napoleon's secretary, who, "in order to preserve the matter secret, translated, and wrote them down in the German language."[2] This was the text that was apparently kept by Napoleon as a "sacred treasure," and which he consulted regularly until he lost it during the Battle of Leipzig in 1813.

However, and unfortunately, since no one was able to translate any ancient Egyptian documents until after Jean François Champollion translated the Rosetta Stone text in 1822, this charming story is unlikely to be true.

According to the translator's preface, the manuscript was found by a Prussian officer who sold it to a French officer. This officer was a prisoner of war who intended to return the manuscript to Napoleon. Unfortunately, he died of injuries he had sustained in battle before he could do this. The manuscript was included in his personal effects that were returned to his family. His family managed to give the manuscript to Empress Marie Louise shortly after Napoleon had been imprisoned on St. Helena. Apparently, she tried to get the manuscript to her husband, without success. After Napoleon's death, she gave Herman Kirchenhoffer permission to translate the book into English.

I am sure Herman Kirchenhoffer would be both surprised and gratified that his book is still in print today.

To use the system described in *The Book of Fate*, the person seeking advice has to make five rows of small upright lines. This is done by making a series of small lines, or dots, in a horizontal row on a sheet of paper, starting at the right-hand side and finishing somewhere near the left-hand side of the page. It is important to take no notice of the number of short lines or dots you are making. Five rows of lines, or dots, need to be made to create the figures used in this system. Each row has to contain at least twelve lines. The number of lines in each row is counted to determine if the total is odd or even.

Lines	Count			
/////////////////	(17)	*		
///////////////	(15)	*		
//////////////	(14)		*	*
///////////////////	(19)	*		
////////////////	(16)		*	*

The instructions state that the five rows of lines are drawn inside a circle containing the twelve signs of the zodiac, using a reed that has been dipped in blood. However, the translator says in a footnote that he and his friends dispensed with the sacrifice and the circle, and obtained good results using pen and ink.

Once the figure has been created, the answer is found in the book. Thirty-two questions can be asked using *The Book of Fate*:

> 1. Inform me of any or of all particulars which relate to the Woman I shall *Marry*.

2. Will the *Prisoner* be released or continue captive?

3. Shall I live to an *Old Age*?

4. Shall I have to *travel* far by Sea or Land, or to reside in foreign Climes?

5. Shall I be involved in *Litigation*, & if so, shall I gain or lose my Cause?

6. Shall I make, or mar, my Fortune by *Gambling*?

7. Shall I ever be able to retire from business with a *Fortune*?

8. Shall I be eminent and meet with *Preferment* in my Pursuits?

9. Shall I be *Successful* in my present undertaking?

10. Shall I ever inherit *Testamentary* property?

11. Shall I spend this year *Happier* than the last?

12. Will my *Name* be *Immortalised* & will posterity applaud it?

13. Will the *Friend* I most reckon upon prove faithful or treacherous?

14. Will the stolen *Property* be recovered & will the *Thief* be detected?

15. What is the aspect of the *Seasons* & what *Political Changes* are likely to take place?

16. Will the *Stranger* soon return from abroad?

17. Will my *Beloved* prove *true* in my absence?

18. Will the *Marriage* about to take place be happy and prosperous?

19. After my death will my *Children* be virtuous & happy?

20. Shall I ever recover from my present *Misfortunes*?

21. Does my *Dream* portent good luck or Misfortune?

22. Will it be my lot to experience great *Vicissitudes* in this Life?

23. Will my reputation be at all, or much, affected by *Calumny*?

24. Inform me of all particulars relating to my future *Husband*?

25. Shall the *Patient* recover from Illness?

26. Does the person whom I love *Love* and regard me?

27. Shall my intended *Journey* be prosperous or unlucky?

28. Shall I ever find a *Treasure*?

29. What *Trade* or *Profession* ought I to follow?

30. Have I any, or many, *Enemies*?

31. Are *Absent Friends* in good health, & what is their present employment?

32. Shall my Wife have a *Son* or a *Daughter*?

The book fails to explain how these questions, and their answers, enabled Napoleon to achieve fame and success. However, there is no doubt whatsoever that Herman Kirchenhoffer achieved financial success from writing, or translating, this book. I own a copy of the sixteenth edition of the book, which was published in 1828, just six years after the book was first published. It originally sold for five shillings, a considerable sum at the time.

Strangely enough, in the same year that *The Book of Fate* was published, another book appeared that also claimed to have helped Napoleon win his various battles. This was *The Philosophical Merlin*, "edited" by Robert Cross Smith (1795–1832) and G. W. Graham. Graham was a celebrated balloonist of his day, and was also interested in astrology and alchemy. Smith was a prolific author, and the first of many astrologers to use the pseudonym "Raphael." He chose this name because the Archangel Raphael has traditionally been associated with the planet Mercury, which is the planetary ruler of astrology. During his lifetime, Smith had a reputation for "discovering" manuscripts that related to Napoleon. *The Philosophical Merlin* was his first publication, and it was not a success. Most of the stock was remaindered.[3] Smith's second book (*The Astrologer of the Nineteenth Century, or Compendium of Astrology, Geomancy and Occult Philosophy*) also failed, but he achieved huge success once he started publishing an annual astrological almanac with predictions for every day of the year called *The Prophetic Messenger*. This almanac is still being published today as *Raphael's Almanac*.

People in England became interested in Napoleon once he died. Napoleon was known to be fascinated with palmistry and may have been interested in astrology as well. Mlle. M. A. Le Normand, a well-known fortuneteller who read Napoleon's hands on a number of occasions, wrote: "On the eve of a battle he [Napoleon] sought to discover the course of the planets in the heavens; like a new Mahomet, he claimed to be able to read in them the issue of combats."[4] Because of Napoleon's interest in psychic matters, it is not surprising that Robert Cross Smith and Herman Kirchenhoffer decided to write books to capitalize on this.

The Philosophical Merlin uses the sixteen figures of geo-mancy. The person thinks of a question while making eight rows of dots on a sheet of paper. There need to be at least twelve dots in each line. These eight rows create two geo-mantic figures. These are combined to create a final figure:

.... (14 dots) ◯ ◯

.... (17 dots) ◯

.... (18 dots) ◯ ◯

.... (15 dots) ◯

.... (17 dots) ◯

.... (16 dots) ◯ ◯

.... (16 dots) ◯ ◯

.... (15 dots) ◯

◯ ◯ + ◯ = ◯

◯ ◯ ◯ ◯

◯ ◯ ◯ ◯ ◯ ◯

◯ ◯ ◯ ◯

Acquisitio + Carcer = Fortuna Minor

In this example, the person reads the entry for Fortuna Minor and, one hopes, finds the answer to his or her question. If not, the text suggests that you repeat the experiment again, after waiting at least one hour. Robert Cross Smith helpfully suggests that it is a good idea to ask the question three times, leaving at least one hour between each try. If the same figure occurs twice or three times, it automatically becomes the figure that is interpreted. However, if all three figures are different, the person can choose which one he or she will use.

conclusion

Until about three hundred years ago, geomancy was considered equally as important as the other major forms of divination. This can be clearly seen in the frontispiece to the second volume of *Utriusque Cosmi, Maioris scilicet et Minoris, metaphysica, physica, atque technica Historia* (1619), by Robert Fludd. Inside a circle are illustrations of the seven main divinatory arts of his time. These were: natural prophecy, geomancy, the Lullian Art of Memory, natal astrology, physiognomy, chiromancy, and pyramid science. This shows how highly geomancy was considered in the seventeenth century. Yet somehow, over the centuries, geomancy almost vanished from sight.

There is no single reason for this, but the popularity of Napoleon's *Book of Fate* and other similar works must have contributed. These books reduced geomancy to a parlor game in which you created a figure and then looked up the answer. The method taught by the Hermetic Order of the Golden Dawn was not much better. These simplistic approaches do nothing to foster an interest in serious geomancy.

When it is utilized correctly, geomancy can provide helpful, useful, and accurate answers to all of life's questions. However, this takes more time and effort than simply looking up an answer.

Fortunately, a handful of people kept geomancy alive, and today it is regaining its lost popularity again. I hope you have created a variety of charts for yourself and discovered how practical and useful geomancy can be. If you practice, experiment, and keep accurate records of your divinations, you'll be able to contribute to the art and help geomancy regain its rightful place as one of the major divination systems in the world.

You'll find geomancy useful in every area of your life. It will amplify and answer your questions, give you new concepts and ideas to consider, and provide you with advice on any subject. If you work professionally as a psychic reader, you'll find geomancy a useful addition to your arsenal, as it will enable you to answer your clients' most specific questions.

I'm sure you'll find geomancy a useful and practical skill, and I wish you great success with it.

notes

Introduction

1. Judith Gleason, *A Recitation of Ifa, Oracle of the Yoruba* (New York: Grossman Publishers, 1973), 13–14.

2. Rolandino da Padova, *Cronica in Factis et Circa Facta Marchie Trivixane.* Article in *The Occult in Medieval Europe 500–1500*, edited and translated by P. G. Maxwell-Stuart (Basingstoke, UK: Palgrave Macmillan, 2005), 84.

3. Donald Tyson, "Geomancy." Appendix VIII in *Three Books of Occult Philosophy, Written by Henry Cornelius Agrippa of Nettesheim* (St. Paul, MN: Llewellyn, 1992), 773.

4. Robert Fludd, *De Geomantia*. The original Latin version is available on several websites.

5. C. H. Josten, "Robert Fludd's Theory of Geomancy and his Experience at Avignon in the Winter of 1601 to 1602." Article in *Journal of the Warburg and Courtald Institutes*, 27, 1964, 327–35.

6. Émile Grillot de Givry (translated by J. Courtenay Locke), *Illustrated Anthology of Sorcery, Magic and Alchemy* (New York: Causeway Books, 1973), 292.

7. Michael Howard, *Modern Wicca: A History From Gerald Gardner to the Present* (Woodbury, MN: Llewellyn, 2010), 57.

8. Dan Brown, *The Lost Symbol* (New York: Doubleday, 2009), 29.

Chapter One

1. Richard Webster, *Feng Shui for Beginners* (St. Paul, MN: Llewellyn, 2002), 1–10.

2. Emilie Savage-Smith and Marion B. Smith, *Islamic Geomancy and a Thirteenth-Century Divinatory Device* (UCLA Studies in Near Eastern Culture and Society, 2), (Malibu, CA: Undena Publications, 1980).

3. Israel Regardie, *Practical Guide to Geomantic Divination* (London: Aquarian Press, 1972), 8.

Chapter Two

1. Richard Wilhelm (translated by C. F. Baynes), *I Ching or Book of Changes* (New York: Pantheon Books, 1964).

Chapter Six

1. The attributions of planets to houses listed here are the traditional geomantic ones. Modern-day astrologers use a different system of attributions: Aries and Mars rule the first house; Taurus and Venus, the second; Gemini and Mercury, the third; Cancer and the Moon, the fourth; Leo and the Sun, the fifth; Virgo and Mercury, the sixth; Libra and Venus, the seventh; Scorpio and Pluto, the eighth; Sagittarius and Jupiter, the ninth; Capricorn and Saturn, the tenth; Aquarius and Uranus, the eleventh; and Pisces and Neptune, the twelfth.

2. Dan Brown, *The Lost Symbol* (New York: Doubleday, 2009), 29.

3. David Ovason, *The Secret Architecture of Our Nation's Capital* (New York: Harper Perennial, 2002).

Chapter Eight

1. Donald Tyson (editor and annotator), *Three Books of Occult Philosophy, Written by Henry Cornelius Agrippa of Nettesheim* (St. Paul, MN: Llewellyn, 1992).

2. Abbot John Trithemius, quoted in *Terrestrial Astrology: Divination by Geomancy* by Stephen Skinner (London: Routledge and Kegan Paul, 1980), 122.

3. The origin of the *Fourth Book of Occult Philosophy* is not known. It was possibly compiled and published by Johann Wierus, an apprentice of Cornelius Agrippa. As well as *Of Geomancy*, by Cornelius Agrippa, this book contains works by Georg Pictorius Villinganus, Gerard of Cremona, and Peter d'Abano.

4. Cornelius Agrippa, quoted in *Three Books of Occult Philosophy, Written by Henry Cornelius Agrippa of Nettesheim*, 773.

5. Cornelius Agrippa, *Of Geomancy*, in *Fourth Book of Occult Philosophy*, 8–9.

6. Cornelius Agrippa, *Of Geomancy*, 8–9.

Chapter Ten

1. Geoffrey of Monmouth, translated by B. Clarke, *Vita Merlini* (Cardiff, UK: University of Wales, 1973).

Chapter Twelve

1. Herman Kirchenhoffer (translator), *The Book of Fate* (London: C. S. Arnold, 1822), vi.

2. Kirchenhoffer, *The Book of Fate*, x.

3. Owen Davies, *Grimoires: A History of Magic Books* (Oxford: Oxford University Press, 2009), 137.

4. Mlle M. A. Le Normand, quoted in Émile Grillot de Givry, *Illustrated Anthology of Sorcery, Magic and Alchemy* (New York: Causeway Books, 1973), 276.

suggested reading

Agrippa, Henry Cornelius. *Fourth Book of Occult Philosophy*. London: Askin Publishers, 1977. (First English publication 1655.)

Agrippa, Henry Cornelius (edited and annotated by Donald Tyson). *Three Books of Occult Philosophy*. St. Paul, MN: Llewellyn, 1992.

Bascom, William. *Ifa Divination: Communication Between Gods and Men in West Africa*. Bloomington: Indiana University Press, 1969.

Cattan, Christopher. *The Geomancy of Master Christopher Cattan*. London: John Wolf, 1591. Reprinted by Antiquus Astrologia, 2007.

Cicero, Chic, and Sandra Tabatha Cicero. *Self-Initiation into the Golden Dawn Tradition*. St. Paul, MN: Llewellyn, 1995.

Crowley, Aleister. *A Handbook of Geomancy*. Sequim, WA: Holmes Publishing Group, reprint, 1989.

Deacon, Richard. *The Book of Fate*. London: Muller and Company, 1976.

Gleason, Judith. *A Recitation of Ifa, Oracle of the Yoruba*. New York: Grossman, 1973.

Greer, John Michael. *The Art and Practice of Geomancy*. San Francisco: Red Wheel/Weiser Books, 2009.

Hartmann, Franz. *Geomancy: A Method of Divination*. Berwick, ME: Ibis Press, 2004. This is a rearranged reprint of *The Principles of Astrological Geomancy*. London: Theosophical Publishing Company, Limited, 1889.

Kirchenhoffer, Herman. *The Book of Fate*. London: C. S. Arnold, 1822.

Lehrich, Christopher I. *The Language of Demons and Angels: Cornelius Agrippa's Occult Philosophy*. Leiden, the Netherlands: Koninklijke Brill, 2003.

Pennick, Nigel. *Games of the Gods*. London: Rider and Company, 1989.

———. *The Oracle of Geomancy: The Divinatory Arts of Raml, Geomantia, Sikidy, and I Ching*. Chieveley, UK: Capall Bann, 1995.

Raphael (pseudonym of Robert Cross Smith). *The Astrologer of the Nineteenth Century, or Compendium of Astrology, Geomancy and Occult Philosophy*. London: Society of the Mercurii, 1825.

Regardie, Israel. *The Golden Dawn: A Complete Course in Practical Ceremonial Magic.* Four Volumes in One. Sixth edition. St. Paul, MN: Llewellyn, 1989.

———. *A Practical Guide to Geomantic Divination.* New York: Samuel Weiser, 1972.

Schwei, Priscilla, and Ralph Pestka. *The Complete Book of Astrological Geomancy.* St. Paul, MN: Llewellyn, 1990.

Skinner, Stephen. *The Complete Magician's Tables.* Singapore: Golden Hoard Press, 2006.

———. *The Oracle of Geomancy: Techniques of Earth Divination.* New York: Warner Books, 1977.

———. *Terrestrial Astrology: Divination by Geomancy.* London: Routledge & Kegan Paul, 1980.

Smith, Robert Cross, and G. W. Graham. *The Philosophical Merlin: Being the Translation of a Valuable Manuscript, Formerly in the Possession of Napoleon Buonaparte.* Part One. London: John Denley, 1822. (Part Two of this book was never published.)

Thomas, Keith. *Religion and the Decline of Magic.* New York: Charles Scribner's Sons, 1971.

Webster, Richard. *Omens, Oghams & Oracles.* St. Paul, MN: Llewellyn, 1995.

index

To Write to the Author

If you wish to contact the author or would like more information about this book, please write to the author in care of Llewellyn Worldwide, and we will forward your request. Both the author and publisher appreciate hearing from you and learning of your enjoyment of this book and how it has helped you. Llewellyn Worldwide cannot guarantee that every letter written to the author can be answered, but all will be forwarded. Please write to:

Richard Webster
℅ Llewellyn Worldwide
2143 Wooddale Drive
Woodbury, MN 55125-2989

Please enclose a self-addressed stamped envelope for reply, or $1.00 to cover costs. If outside the USA, enclose an international postal reply coupon.